The Puerto Rican Migrant
in New York City

The Puerto Rican Migrant
in New York City

By

LAWRENCE R. CHENAULT

WITH A FOREWORD BY
Francesco Cordasco
MONTCLAIR STATE COLLEGE

NEW YORK / RUSSELL & RUSSELL

325.272
C42p

COPYRIGHT, 1938, BY COLUMBIA UNIVERSITY PRESS
COPYRIGHT RENEWED, 1966, BY LAWRENCE R. CHENAULT
REISSUED, 1970, BY RUSSELL & RUSSELL
A DIVISION OF ATHENEUM PUBLISHERS, INC.
BY ARRANGEMENT WITH COLUMBIA UNIVERSITY PRESS
L. C. CATALOG CARD NO: 74-102477
PRINTED IN THE UNITED STATES OF AMERICA

FOREWORD

LAWRENCE R. CHENAULT'S *The Puerto Rican Migrant in New York City* (1938) was presented as a doctoral dissertation at Columbia University;[1] its importance is twofold: as an early study it is a bibliographical watershed of materials not easily available, and beyond its value both as a commentary on the early migrant experience and a collection of invaluable data, it concerns itself with the problems of housing, of health, and social adjustment for Puerto Ricans, all of which have a critical and continuing importance. Chenault divides his study into two parts. Part I considers "Puerto Rico as a Source of Migration to the United States"; and Part II studies "The Puerto Rican Worker and His Family in New York." A wealth of statistical data is collected, and valuable schema constructed, all of which Chenault assembled with great care and much of which is nowhere else collectively gathered (at the time of Chenault's writing there was no separate enumeration for Puerto Ricans in the Census); and the annotated bibliography (pp. 175-180) is an excellent register of the important literature available in the late 1930s.[2]

The perceptivity of Chenault's observations is everywhere evident, and (allowing for the date of its writing) the following extract from his *Summary* has a clear, if not prophetic, relevancy:

"From the standpoint of the community, certain effects of the migration are clear. As a rule the migrant can satisfy only the demand for unskilled work. In addition to this, the Puerto Rican worker is not as familiar with American customs as is the American-born Negro, and does not have the Negro's ability to speak English. He suffers the same language handicap, usually has less skill, faces a greater adjustment on account of climate and differences in environment, and lacks the physical strength of the majority of the European immigrant stocks. Since there is already a pressing demand for slum clearance in Harlem and in other neighborhoods where the Puerto Ricans have a tendency to concentrate, the migration of a very large number of people from the crowded districts of the island could easily complicate still further the housing and neighborhood situations already existing in these areas. In some respects, the migration of the Puerto Rican has had the same effect upon the community health conditions as that of the Negro. The apparent susceptibility of the Puerto Rican to tuberculosis and the incidence of this disease among them is much greater than that found among the American-born colored groups. Parasitical diseases present a special health problem arising out of the migration. As with the influx of Southern Negroes, there are other problems of crime, education, race contacts, and even some with political aspects. Because of the difference in culture and the environment which has conditioned the migrant before his arrival in this country, practically the same problem of assimilation exists for the Puerto Rican as for the non-citizen immigrant groups. To the extent that the Puerto Rican feels that the American occupation of his native island has resulted in an encroachment upon his own culture, and to the extent that he therefore retains the attitudes which result from and go with an aroused nationalism among his people, this problem of assimilation will be made more difficult." (pp. 158-159)

And his observations on the educational problems posed by Puerto Rican children (again, remembering that it was written in the late 1930s) have all the earmarks of contemporary discussion:

"Not only does the low economic status of the worker affect his ability to overcome rapidly his lack of skill and training, but the poverty of the family appears to have a definite relation to the success of the worker's children in the public schools. Although Puerto Ricans as a rule profess to be Catholics, they do not send their children to parochial schools. Many Puerto Rican children who enter the public schools in New York speak or understand little English. The children who are transferred from schools in Puerto Rico to those in New York are usually put back in their classes so that they are with children who are two or three years younger than they are. Americans who are teaching Puerto Rican children express the opinion that these children have had less training in discipline and in group cooperation than American children. Lacking the timidity of many of the children in this country, they sometimes act in an unrestrained and impulsive manner. One large agency in the settlement, which has dealt with Puerto Rican children for many years, reported that under proper conditions Puerto Rican children are responsive, easily managed, and affectionate. In contrast to this, another large institution said that for some reason which they could not explain, the Puerto Rican children were more destructive than any group of children with whom they had had contact. All the evidence obtainable shows the relation of unsatisfactory home conditions to difficulties at school. During the past few years the desperate economic condition of these families has caused them to move so frequently that it has often been difficult to locate the children when they did not attend school." (p. 146)

In essence, Chenault's study graphically attested to the problems implicit in the vast migrations which were changing the character of American cities; and which were combining to bring urban poverty to national attention in a guise in which the Puerto Ricans were only one component of pervasive patterns of socio-economic deprivation, and only one group among the contemporary poor whom the Economic Opportunity Act "discovered" in 1964. Much of what Chenault has to say could become part of any of our contemporary tracts on urban poverty, and the currency of his animadversions underscores the continuation of the concerns: *e.g.*, "The social adjustment necessitated by the migration results from the abrupt change of people but slightly removed from the peasant class from a simple rural environment to the slum section of an enormous city. The migration causes disintegrating forces to affect the family. In addition to this painful adjustment, the worker and his family are exposed to conditions which have long been recognized as harmful to the happiness and well-being of all people regardless of background. Often mixed with other families under extremely crowded conditions, without funds or employment, and in many cases suffering from malnutrition or some chronic disease, it is not strange that the worker and his family feel the influence of the antisocial behavior which is prevalent in these neighborhoods. Having come from an island where he has already acquired a feeling of mistreatment at the hands of the American people and their government, he is often resentful as a result of the clash in culture, racial antagonisms, and the failure to realize many expectations because of what he feels are discrimination and indifference." (pp. 157-158)

It is hardly necessary to point out that much of Chenault's language and phraseology are somewhat dated (if not abrasive) to our new and heightened sensitivities, and that his Puerto Rican vignettes are at times seemingly caricatured (as his reference to American blacks as "colored" is incongruous in the late 1960s), but there is, despite these *contretemps*, no diminution in the value of his work.[3]

---

[1]"Advanced graduate research on Puerto Rico in American universities was negligible during the first forty years of this century, with a total of 26 dissertations being completed, 18 of which were accepted during the 1930s. The next decade produced 42 titles. The marked acceleration in output with more than 250 dissertations being accepted since 1950 is a reflection of growth in doctoral research everywhere." Jesse J. Dossick, *Doctoral Research on Puerto Rico and*

Puerto Ricans (New York: New York University Press, 1967). This pamphlet lists 320 doctoral dissertations dealing with Puerto Rico and Puerto Ricans completed and accepted in universities on the mainland.

[2]Some of Chenault's entries have a special interest, *e.g.*, Robert F. Foerster, *The Racial Problems Involved in Immigration from Latin America and the West Indies to the United States* (Washington: U.S. Department of Labor, Government Printing Office, 1926), of which Chenault observes: "The thesis of this study is that immigration from these countries represents an adverse selection for the United States on account of the large Negro and Indian elements in their populations." Foerster was the historian of Italian immigration. See Robert F. Foerster, *The Italian Emigration of Our Times*, with A New Introductory Note by F. Cordasco (New York: Russell & Russell, 1968) [Originally, Harvard University Press, 1919].

[3]A vast bibliography on Puerto Ricans in the United States is being assembled; see F. Cordasco and E. Bucchioni, *Puerto Rican Children In Mainland Schools: A Source Book For Teachers* (New York: Scarecrow Press, 1968) which is a sociological sourcebook and goes far beyond the limitations of its title, and includes a bibliography of some 450 items. The statistical indices of Puerto Rican urban poverty (and the related needs) are best assembled in *The Puerto Rican Community Development Project* (New York: The Puerto Rican Forum, 1964); and a review of much of the literature is available in "Puerto Rican Migrants on the Mainland of the United States," *IRCD Bulletin*, vol. IV (January, 1968). The vast portraits of *Kulturpessimismus* and decadence (the "culture of poverty" concept) of Oscar Lewis, *La Vida: A Puerto Rican Family in the Culture of Poverty* (New York: Random House, 1966), and *A Study of Slum Culture: Backgrounds For La Vida* (New York: Random House, 1968) should be read with reference to a contrary view in F. Cordasco, "Another Face of Poverty: Oscar Lewis' La Vida," *Phylon: The Atlanta Review of Race & Culture*, vol. 29 (Spring, 1968), pp. 88-92, and the detailed notices of *La Vida* by Gertrude S. Goldberg and Edmund W. Gordon in *IRCD Bulletin*, noted *supra*. For the East Harlem (New York City) Puerto Rican subcommunity experience, see Don Wakefield, *Island in the City* (Boston: Houghton Mifflin, 1959); Elena Padilla, *Up from Puerto Rico* (New York: Columbia University Press, 1958); and Patricia Sexton, *Spanish Harlem: Anatomy of Poverty* (New York: Harper & Row, 1965), with references to the article-review, F. Cordasco, "Nights in the Gardens of East Harlem: Patricia Sexton's *East Harlem*," *Journal of Negro Education*, vol. 34 (Fall, 1965), pp. 450-451; and for notices of ethnic subcommunities in East Harlem (Irish, Jewish, Italian, Negro, and Puerto Rican), see F. Cordasco and Rocco Galatioto, "Ethnic Displacement in the Interstitial Community: The East Harlem (New York City) Experience," *Kansas Journal of Sociology*, vol. V, #2 (Spring, 1969). The Puerto Rican educational experience on the mainland is best studied in F. Cordasco and E. Bucchioni, *op. cit.*; and in the monumental study undertaken by the New York City Board of Education, J. Cayce Morrison, director, *The Puerto Rican Study* (1953-1957): *A Report on the Education and Adjustment of Puerto Rican Pupils in the Public Schools of the City of New York* (New York: Board of Education, 1958). *The Summary of Recommendations Made by the Puerto Rican Study* is reprinted in F. Cordasco and E. Bucchioni, *op. cit.* Not to be neglected is the autobiography of Leonard Covello, *The Heart is the Teacher* (New York: McGraw-Hill, 1958) which recounts Covello's long tenure as Principal of Benjamin Franklin High School in East Harlem. Invalu-

able memoranda and reports by Dr. Covello on the education of Puerto Rican children are published in F. Cordasco and E. Bucchioni, *op. cit.* A graphic picture of the Puerto Rican educational experience is in Richard J. Margolis, *The Losers: A Report on Puerto Ricans and the Public Schools* (New York: Aspira, 1968). The best source on Puerto Rican migration is the Migration Division of the Department of Labor, Commonwealth of Puerto Rico, which publishes at intervals *A Summary in Facts and Figures: Progress in Puerto Rico—Puerto Rican Migration.* General references include Christopher Rand, *The Puerto Ricans* (New York: Oxford, 1958); Oscar Handlin, *The Newcomers: Negroes and Puerto Ricans in a Changing Metropolis* (Cambridge: Harvard University Press, 1959); Jesus Cólon, *A Puerto Rican in New York and Other Sketches* (New York: Mainstream Publications, 1961); Nathan Glazer and Daniel P. Moynihan, *Beyond the Melting Pot: The Negroes, Puerto Ricans, Jews, Italians, and Irish of New York City* (Cambridge: M.I.T. Press, 1963); Clarence Senior, *The Puerto Ricans* (Chicago: Quadrangle Books, 1965). A special issue of *The International Migration Review* (Spring, 1968) is devoted to the Puerto Rican experience on the United States mainland.

FRANCESCO CORDASCO

CONSULTANT, MIGRATION DIVISION
COMMONWEALTH OF PUERTO RICO

Montclair State College
October, 1969

Preface

WHEN I was teaching in the Department of Economics at the University of Puerto Rico, I became interested in the population problem of the island. Upon discovering that others who had lived on the island for many years and had long experience with the Puerto Rican people were planning to write on this subject, I thought it best to leave the development of such a treatise to students who might be better qualified for the task.

The present study might be considered a continuation or outgrowth of the preliminary work on the population problem of Puerto Rico. It was apparent that the migration of a large number of Puerto Ricans to New York and other northern centers could easily have important social consequences for these particular areas. As studies about almost all of the other cultural groups had already been made, it seemed that one about the Puerto Rican migrant in New York might find a place alongside those about the Filipinos, the Hawaiians, and the Mexicans.

The choice of this subject for a dissertation was not made without full appreciation of the difficulties that would handicap the work. The problem of sources and the limitations which would be encountered in making a study of this kind were apparent from the very beginning.

The reader will realize my indebtedness to many individuals for information about the Puerto Rican worker in New York. I found social workers, nurses, and members of the staffs of a great variety of institutions always glad to give me their time and to assist me wherever possible. Dr. Sophia Robison of the Welfare Council and Miss Marguerite Potter of the New York City Department of Health furnished me with unpublished data from the census and with other information. Dr. H. R. Edwards of the Department of Health has been particularly helpful. Thanks are also due to the Honorable William Hodson of the Department of Public Welfare of New York City, to various members of his staff, and to Mr. J. M. Vivaldi of the Department of Labor of Puerto Rico. Professor Ira de A Reid added one or two interesting facts about the racial relations of the various cultural groups in the Harlem section.

To my friend and former teacher, Professor Robert E. Chaddock of the Department of Sociology of Columbia University, I am heavily indebted. He lent a word of encouragement to the undertaking in the beginning, and continued to furnish me with numerous suggestions and helpful criticisms throughout its preparation. Dr. Joseph Dorfman, who acted as a representative of the Department of Economics, also read the manuscript. My wife helped me to find some of the information about the Puerto Rican people both on the island and in New York, and assisted in the preparation of the manuscript.

L. R. C.

Hunter College, New York
March 15, 1938

Contents

I. INTRODUCTION 1

Introductory Statement.—History and definition of problem.—Its significance.—Nature and purpose of study.—Sources and their limitations

PART ONE

Puerto Rico as a Source of Migration to the United States

II. RESOURCES, INDUSTRIES, AND POLITICAL STATUS OF THE ISLAND 11

Geography.—Land resources and agriculture.—Mineral resources and industrialization.—Present government and the movement for independence

III. COMPOSITION, GROWTH, AND ECONOMIC CONDITIONS OF THE POPULATION OF PUERTO RICO 23

THE POPULATION

Composition.—Puerto Rico still largely rural.—Occupations.—Puerto Rico a country with a large proportion of children.—Growth.—Natural increase by growing excess of births.—Density

ECONOMIC AND LIVING CONDITIONS

Wages.—Housing.—Health conditions on the island.—Education.—Economic distress aggravated by the depression.—Pressure of population upon resources and its consequences

TWO MAIN ALTERNATIVES FOR RELIEVING POPULATION PRESSURE
The outlook for birth control.—Migration as an alternative

IV. THE MOVEMENT OF THE PUERTO RICAN TO THE UNITED STATES 51

Motives for migration.—Ease of movement.—Size and year of movement.—Places of settlement.—Immediate adjustments for the Puerto Rican migrant who moves to New York.—Sex and color of the migrants.—Social classes represented.—The concentration of the Puerto Rican in certain areas of New York City

PART TWO

The Puerto Rican Worker and His Family in New York

V. OCCUPATIONS AND EMPLOYMENT OPPORTUNITIES   69

Where and how the migrant finds work.—Handicaps in obtaining work.—Other factors related to employment.—The migrant's poor economic status as shown by dependency.—Summary and conclusion

VI. THE HOUSING OF THE PUERTO RICAN WORKER IN NEW YORK CITY   89

Area in Harlem with large Puerto Rican population.—General characteristics of housing in the selected area of Harlem.—Evidence of crowding as shown by size of families and the practice of families living together.—The Brooklyn area.—General characteristics of housing in the Brooklyn settlement.—Summary and conclusion

VII. THE PROBLEM OF HEALTH   110

Health center districts.—Tuberculosis among the Puerto Ricans in New York.—Parasitical diseases.—General health conditions among the group.—The problem of diet.—Summary

VIII. SOCIAL ADJUSTMENT IN THE NEW COMMUNITY   127

A closer view of the Harlem settlement of Puerto Ricans.—Social maladjustment; crime and delinquency in the community and among the group.—Disintegrating influences affecting the family.—The need for vocational training.—Recreational and social outlets.—The migrant's reaction to religious and political influences

IX. GENERAL SUMMARY AND CONCLUSION   156

APPENDICES

   A. Notes on Method and Materials Used in the Selection of Areas Having a Large Puerto Rican Population   163

   B. Data on Residential and Dwelling Units for Selected Areas in New York City   167

   C. Boundaries and Census Tracts in the Settlements Studied   170

BIBLIOGRAPHY   173

INDEX   181

Figures

1. Area of Puerto Rican Settlement in Harlem, by Census Tracts — 93
2. Settlement of Spanish-speaking Racial Groups in the Lower Harlem Area, New York City — 95
3. Area of Puerto Rican Settlement in Brooklyn, by Census Tracts — 105
4. Mortality Rates of Harlem Health Areas with Large Puerto Rican Population — 113
5. Percent of 10,173 Persons in Harlem Found by X-ray to Have Tuberculosis, New York City, 1933 — 118
6. Areas 8A and 6 of Halpern Study of Crime — 132

Tables

1. The Total Area and Cultivated Land of Puerto Rico in Relation to Its Population in 1933 — 13
2. Acres of Land per Capita and Acres of Improved Land per Capita in Puerto Rico and in Other Countries — 13
3. Urban and Rural Population of Puerto Rico: 1935, 1930, and 1920 — 25
4. Gainfully Occupied Workers in Puerto Rico in 1930 by Important Occupational Classifications — 27
5. The Age Composition of the Population of Puerto Rico and the United States in 1930 — 28
6. Population of Puerto Rico, 1765 to 1935 — 29
7. Annual Rate of Population Growth in Puerto Rico in Selected Periods, 1877–1935 — 30
8. Population Density of Puerto Rico Compared with That of Other Countries — 32
9. Comparison of Wages in Puerto Rico and Continental United States — 34
10. Average Earnings per Week of Workers in Puerto Rico in the Fiscal Year 1933–34 — 35
11. Number of Persons per Room in 4,268 Rural Houses in Puerto Rico — 38
12. Death Rate for Selected Diseases in Puerto Rico in 1935 — 40
13. Number of Persons Born in Puerto Rico and Living in the Continental United States at Census Dates and in 1935 — 53
14. Movement of U. S. Citizens between Puerto Rico and the Continental United States, 1921–35 — 54
15. Persons Born in Puerto Rico and Living in the Continental United States, by Geographical Divisions and States, 1930 and 1920 — 57
16. Persons Born in Puerto Rico and Living in New York City, by Boroughs and Color, 1930 — 63

17. Number of Persons Born in Puerto Rico and Living in New York City in 1930, by Important Statistical Areas   64
18. Placement of Puerto Ricans by the Puerto Rican Employment Service, 1930–36   74
19. Number of Families According to Size, by Census Tracts of Harlem Settlement   103
20. Mortality Rates and New Case Registration in Manhattan and Brooklyn, 1929–33   112
21. Mortality Rates for the Five-Year Period 1929–33   114
22. Pulmonary Tuberculosis Mortality in New York City, 1930-31   116
23. X-ray Diagnoses of 7,140 Individuals in Harlem   117
24. Children Referred as Delinquent in New York City in 1930   136
25. Analysis of Offenses of 493 Delinquent Children in Six Health Areas with a Large Puerto Rican Population   138

Introduction

Chapter I

Introduction

IMPORTANT movements of people from one part of the country to another have taken place from time to time ever since the United States was first settled. This phase of our population problem is one which is receiving increased attention, and numerous studies have recently been made of the migration of particular groups. The number of Puerto Ricans who have come to New York and other cities has now become of sufficient importance to justify study as a part of this larger problem of migration. Since Puerto Rico is a part of the United States and Puerto Ricans are citizens, the movement in a technical sense is one of internal migration. Practically, however, it is much more like one of immigration than migration.

The mass of Puerto Ricans have come to this country since 1920. The migration of the Puerto Rican to New York is a part of a general migration of people to urban centers which was started by the demand for industrial labor created by the World War and which was stimulated in later years by the restriction of immigration. Before the year 1910, there were few Puerto Ricans in the United States. The number continued to be comparatively small up to the 1920 census. The census of 1930 showed that there were between four and five times as many Puerto Ricans living in the United States as there had been in 1920. Although a small number returned to the island during the depression, migration has continued to the present time; and Puerto Ricans now constitute an important group of people in certain sections of New York City.

From the migration of the Puerto Rican to a city such as New York, two problems arise. One involves the Puerto Rican himself, and the other the community in which he settles. The migrant's problem is brought about by an abrupt change from the environment of a rural and tropical island to that of a complicated industrial city. He is a citizen of the United States, but the adjustment required of him in New York is in almost every way equivalent to that of a person who moves from a foreign country to the United States. Climate, language, employment, housing conditions, racial relations—almost every important aspect of his former way of living—are now suddenly changed. In many ways, the movement of the Puerto Rican to New York may be compared to the migration of the Negro from the South to Northern industrial centers; in other ways, there are striking similarities to the social effect of the settlement of the Mexican in American cities.[1] As with other groups of people who have moved to the large cities, the complete environmental change of the Puerto Rican necessitates adjustments out of which social problems arise. It has been found that the migration of large numbers of Negroes or Mexicans from rural communities to certain concentrated areas of the larger cities often affects the labor situation or causes problems of housing, health, and crime. Similar community problems could arise from the settlement of large numbers of Puerto Ricans in New York City.

The present significance of the problem lies not so much in the number of Puerto Ricans now residing in this country as in the fact that the migration from the island to New York will be greatly accelerated in the near future. The past migration from the island constitutes only a small beginning of the migration which will soon take place.

The problem also deserves study on account of the fact that there is a strong tendency for the Puerto Rican to settle in the Harlem section of New York City. About one-half of all the Puerto Ricans living in the United States in 1930 resided in this area. Probably no section of an American city presents more complicated social problems than does this one. The prospect of a greatly increased settlement in this area during the next few years, in addition to the large numbers of Puerto Ricans, Negroes, and other racial groups now living there, makes the study of the movement important.

[1] For an excellent study of the migration of the Negro, see Louise V. Kennedy, *The Negro Peasant Turns Cityward*. Important studies of the Mexican worker in the United States have been made by Paul S. Taylor under the title *Mexican Labor in the United States*, "University of California Publications in Economics," University of California Press, Berkeley, California.

Introduction

Another reason for studying the Puerto Rican migration may be found in the recent agitation on the part of the Puerto Rican people for independence. So long as the island remains a territory of the United States, Puerto Ricans will, as citizens, be free to enter the United States without restriction. Undoubtedly, the question of restriction of immigration from Puerto Rico would arise if complete independence were granted, and a study of the migration which has already taken place would have an important bearing on this problem.

The main purpose of this study of the Puerto Rican migrant in New York is to show some of the social effects resulting from the migration. Its purpose is also to show that a large increase in the population of Puerto Rico will result in a further movement of people from the island to New York, and to suggest some of the problems which such a movement might entail. This study deals with Puerto Rico itself only insofar as the island is a necessary background both for the causes which bring about the migration and for an understanding of the qualities and previous environment of the people who come. Data are given to support the opinion that the movement of people from the island is likely to be much larger in future years than in the past. After a discussion of the background of the migration, its size and the places of settlement in the United States are taken up. This background and discussion of the movement of people make up Part One of the present study. Part Two, which deals with the Puerto Rican worker and his family in New York City, begins with his occupations, employment, and economic status, and continues with a discussion of the housing and health of Puerto Ricans in New York. Other problems dealing with the social adjustments confronting the worker and his family in the new community are then considered. This discussion includes such topics as antisocial behavior, the effect of the migration upon the family, and recreation and social activities.

There are few published sources from which information about the migration can be obtained. Although numerous studies have been made which treat of the social and economic problems of Puerto Rico, nothing has been published about the migration of the Puerto Rican to New York or about his life in this urban environment.² The movement of people and the places of settlement in the United States have been determined from census reports and other data obtained from the United States Department of Labor. The reports of a division of the Department of Labor of Puerto Rico located in New York constitute the most important single source of information about employment and occupations of the worker in New York. Data about dependency have been obtained from the Emergency Relief Bureau of New York City. A discussion of the method and materials used in the selection of the parts of the city in which the Puerto Ricans live is included in Appendix A. Information about housing conditions in these areas has been taken almost entirely from the published report of the New York Housing Authority, *Real Property Inventory*. Reports of the Department of Health of New York City are the source of a major part of the information given about health problems among the group. In the absence of data of a statistical nature, a considerable part of the information has come from institutions, from social workers, and from personal interviews with people who are in close contact with the group in New York. A few unpublished reports have been obtained from institutions which deal directly with the Puerto Rican people in New York. Newspapers, although they have not been treated as sources of information where more authoritative data were available, have furnished the writer with information about the Puerto Ricans which could not have been obtained elsewhere.

The author realizes the limitations of this monograph, and that many important phases of the problem have been omitted or not adequately treated. No attempt has been made to trace by the method of case study particular individuals or families who have moved from the island to New York. The work of the social agency among the Puerto Ricans in New York is another important and difficult subject which had to be dealt with only as a small part of the general problem. This study is intended to be a beginning,

---

² The following are valuable studies dealing with Puerto Rico: V. S. Clark and Associates, *Porto Rico and Its Problems;* K. Mixer, *Porto Rico, History and Conditions, Social, Economic, and Political;* B. W. and J. W. Diffie, *Porto Rico, A Broken Pledge;* J. Enamorado-Cuesta, *Porto Rico Past and Present.* A useful survey of the entire Caribbean area is given by C. L. Jones in *Caribbean Backgrounds and Prospects.*

rather than a full and complete study of the Puerto Rican migration. The failure to treat many important aspects of the problem adequately is to be explained in part by the previously mentioned lack of available material on the subject. The sources of material are especially limited as to the demographical features of the migration. Except for one pamphlet study connected with the results of mental tests administered to Puerto Rican school children nothing has been published about the Puerto Ricans in New York.[3] There are practically no articles in current periodical literature which deal directly with the Puerto Rican migrant in Harlem. This study attempts to assemble for the first time what material is now available about the movement of the Puerto Rican to New York and his life here.

Before discussing the migration of the Puerto Rican to New York, it is necessary to go back to Puerto Rico and to study the life on the island. This background, which is necessary for an understanding and appreciation of the problem and its significance, will be discussed in the following chapter. It is important for two main reasons: first, to understand the conditions which cause the migration and which may greatly accelerate it in the future; and second, to know more about the type of persons who come and their previous conditioning on the island.

[3] C. P. Armstrong and Associates, *Reaction of Puerto Rican Children in New York City to Psychological Tests.*

PART ONE

Puerto Rico as a Source of Migration to the United States

CHAPTER II

Resources, Industries, and Political Status of the Island

THE MIGRATION from Puerto Rico, unlike the movement of people from any of the South American countries and from all but a few of the islands of the West Indies, is closely related to the island's population problem. In order to explain the significance of this problem to migration, this chapter discusses in a brief way the island's land and mineral resources, its dependence upon outside resources for food, and its industrial development. When these facts have been presented and related to the size, growth, and economic condition of the island's population, discussed in Chapter III, the problem facing the Puerto Rican in his native island and the importance of the economic conditions found there to the study of migration will be made clear.

GEOGRAPHY

Puerto Rico is a rectangular island somewhat smaller than the state of Connecticut, averaging about thirty-five miles in width and one hundred miles in length and containing a little more than 3,400 square miles.[1] It is situated about 1,420 miles southeast of New York, 1,000 miles east of Havana, and 500 miles north of Venezuela. To the west of Puerto Rico lies Santo Domingo; and to the east lie the Virgin Islands.

Topographically, Puerto Rico is the top of a partially submerged mountain range. As one approaches the island for the first time, he is attracted by the curious shape of the "haystack" hills which stand out against the horizon and which are accounted for by the

[1] The name of Porto Rico was changed to Puerto Rico, the correct name of the island in Spanish, by an Act of Congress, May 17, 1932. A summary of the important facts about the geography and climate of the island will be found in Mixer, *op. cit.*, Chapter I. See also J. E. McCord, *Types of Farming in Puerto Rico.*

volcanic origin of the island. A range of mountains, which extends east and west in about the center of the island, reaches an altitude of from 3,500 to 4,000 feet. As the trade winds blow from the north or northeast, the contact of moisture-laden winds causes a wet and a dry belt. Rainfall, which averages seventy-one inches, varies greatly in different parts of the island. In some of the mountainous sections, it may, for some years, exceed 140 inches, while in other areas there is so little rainfall that irrigation is required.

Although Puerto Rico is definitely tropical in climate and vegetation, the cool Atlantic trade winds which blow almost continuously throughout the year greatly relieve the oppressive heat which would normally exist in regions of this latitude, and cause the climate to be, though warm, one of the most healthful in the tropics. The mean annual temperature, although varying somewhat with altitude, is seventy-six degrees. The annual average variation in temperature between the summer and winter months is about ten degrees. Puerto Rico is in the hurricane zone, and has had numerous destructive storms in the course of its history.

LAND RESOURCES AND AGRICULTURE

One important factor which can cause migration from a country as crowded as Puerto Rico is the lack of natural resources to support its growing population. Of primary importance among the natural resources of a country are the amount, quality, and availability of land.

In Puerto Rico at the present time there is a scarcity of land to produce food for the people, much less to provide for future growth. With a total area of approximately 2,200,000 acres and a population of slightly over 1,700,000 people, there is only about one and one-third acres of total land area per capita.[2] Table 1 shows the land resources of the island in relation to its population. Since one-half of the entire area is estimated to be improved land, there is only about three-fourths of an acre of improved land per person.[3]

[2] The population on December 1, 1935, was 1,723,534, and the density per square mile at this date was 507. See pp. 29 and 32.

[3] The actual figure for improved land according to the 1930 census was 1,220,000 acres. See McCord, *op. cit.*, p. 29. The Census Bureau defines improved land as follows: "Under this heading are reported all land regularly tilled or mowed; land in pastures that has been cleared or tilled; land lying fallow; land in gardens and

The 660,000 acres in cultivation represent a little more than one-third of an acre per person.

Table 1. THE TOTAL AREA AND CULTIVATED LAND OF PUERTO RICO IN RELATION TO ITS POPULATION IN 1933

Land in cultivation (sugar cane, coffee, tobacco, fruits, and other crops)	657,468 acres (30%)
Noncultivated land	1,540,932 acres (70%)
Pasturage, 1,044,698 acres (48%)	
Woods, marshes, and other land, 496,234 acres (22%)	
Total area	2,198,400 acres
Population (estimate)	1,700,000
Persons per square mile	495
Persons per cultivated square mile	1,654

Source: D. DeGolia, *Tariff Problems of Puerto Rico*, a report of the Tariff Survey Division of the Puerto Rican Emergency Relief Administration, Bureau of Supplies, Printing, and Transportation, San Juan, 1935, p. 69.

Puerto Rico's great shortage of land is revealed by a comparison of its land per capita with that of other countries, as shown in Table 2. Although Puerto Rico is almost entirely agricultural, the amount of improved land per person is about the same as that of Italy and Germany. It has less land per capita than most of the highly industrialized European nations.

Table 2. ACRES OF LAND PER CAPITA AND ACRES OF IMPROVED LAND PER CAPITA IN PUERTO RICO AND IN OTHER COUNTRIES

Country	Acres per Capita	Acres of Improved Land per Capita
Puerto Rico	1.42	.79
United States	15.77	2.08
Hawaii	11.13	1.20
Cuba	7.50	—
Philippine Islands	6.06	3.28
France	3.25	1.32
Denmark	2.98	1.86
Italy	1.82	.81
Germany	1.80	.79

Source: *Types of Farming in Puerto Rico*, p. 22.

The rugged and mountainous topography of Puerto Rico greatly limits the land available for cultivation. About three-quarters of

---

orchards; and land occupied by buildings and barnyards." Source, *Fifteenth Census of U. S.* (1930), *Outlying Territories and Possessions*, p. 205.

the entire surface of the island is broken and irregular.[4] Of the several topographic sections defined in the agricultural surveys, the mountainous section covers more than one-half of the total area of the island.[5] About thirty percent of the total area is already in cultivated crops and more than one-half of the total area has been improved.[6] At this time there is only a comparatively small amount of land left which could be put into cultivation.

The system of land tenure in Puerto Rico is a factor which greatly accentuates its scarcity of agricultural land. As is well known, sugar cane is by far the most important crop of the island.[7] With the development of the sugar industry, there has come a plantation system and a concentration of land in large farms. The 1930 census showed that there were 52,965 farms in Puerto Rico. About 71 percent or 37,587 of these farms were under twenty acres in size. The many small farms of under twenty acres, however, contained only fifteen percent of all the improved land on the island. On the other hand, farms of over 500 acres in size, or .7 percent of the total number, accounted for 34 percent of the total improved land.[8] Many peasants, having sold the land which they could now use for the growing of subsistence crops for their families, have become landless agricultural workers.

In Puerto Rico, the present leading crops—sugar cane, tobacco, and coffee—were important long before the American occupation.[1] After the occupation, sugar cane has each year come more and more into prominence as the money crop of the island.[9] The growing of sugar cane in Puerto Rico is a good example of specialization

[4] Mixer, *op. cit.*, p. 5; Diffie, *op. cit.*, p. 163.
[5] McCord, *op. cit.*, p. 7.
[6] *Ibid.*, p. 21.
[7] The sugar industry is responsible for more than one-half of the island's exports and about one-half of the island's wealth. Approximately one-half of the entire land in cultivation is used for growing sugar cane. See Diffie, *op. cit.*, p. 201.
[8] McCord, *op. cit.*, p. 22. The so-called "500-acre law" enacted by Congress soon after Puerto Rico became a part of the United States, which prohibits the holding of land in excess of 500 acres by a corporation engaged in agriculture, has been evaded by means of various legal devices and has never been effective.
[9] It is estimated that the total investment of foreign capital in the island amounts, at the present time, to about $125,000,000. For the most part, this sum is American capital. The approximate divisions of the investments have been given as follows: sugar enterprises, $30,000,000; fruit enterprises, $1,000,000; utilities, $8,500,000; insular, municipal, and private debts, $70,500,000; and importing establishments, banks, and miscellaneous, $15,000,000. See DeGolia, *op. cit.*, p. 49.

Resources of the Island

in agriculture and is similar to the development which has taken place in Cuba. Many Puerto Ricans point to this development as the main source of their economic problem. Since the cost of production of sugar in Puerto Rico is much higher than in Cuba and other sugar-producing areas, like Louisiana and the areas which produce American beet sugar, the industry is dependent on tariff protection.[10] During the last ten years the production of sugar has more than doubled; it now exceeds a million tons per year. Tobacco, which is an important export crop of Puerto Rico, has always suffered the keenest competition. A large part of the tobacco is exported to be used as filler for cigars. Coffee, at one time the most important crop, now ranks third. It is the crop of the higher altitudes and the cooler parts of the island. In the matter of price, but not in quality, Puerto Rican coffee is at a great disadvantage with the South American coffee. The United States has never been an important market for Puerto Rican coffee and for the most part growers of coffee have exported their surplus to the markets of Europe. Production in recent years has shown a serious decline because many trees were destroyed by the hurricanes of 1928 and 1932. Citrus fruit cultivation is comparatively a new venture in Puerto Rico, having been introduced since the American occupation, and it is largely in the hands of American farmers. At one time it was thought that cotton might become an important crop of the island, but its production has declined rapidly because of low prices and insects.

The facts already given about the small amount of land for the

[10] As Cuba is by far the most important competitor of Puerto Rico, the protection given to the latter on sugar depends on the preferential tariff rate for Cuba, rather than the general tariff rate. For example, in 1933, the general rate per pound was $.025, and the rate for Cuba was $.02. Under these conditions, Puerto Rico would not be able to compete in the American market without tariff protection. Although wages in sugar production were from 60 to 85 cents per day in Puerto Rico, 40 to 60 cents in Cuba, and as low as 20 cents in Santo Domingo, the cost of production in Cuba was lower than in Santo Domingo, and was only about one-third that of Puerto Rico: the estimated cost of production per pound of sugar, 1931-32, in Puerto Rico was $.0275, and in Cuba was $.0076. The tariff benefit to Puerto Rico in dollars, Cuba's preferential rate multiplied by the number of pounds shipped to the United States by Puerto Rico, amounted to about $33,000,000 in such years as 1932-33 and 1933-34. The benefit in later years (for example, the preferential rate for Cuba in 1935 was $.009) cannot be measured by Cuba's preferential rate on account of the restriction of Cuban sugar and the quota system for crops in Puerto Rico. See DeGolia, *op. cit.*, pp. 27 and 47; see also Diffie, *op. cit.*, Chapter VII.

island's population show the difficulty of building up subsistence crops. The *jíbaro* is usually allowed by the landlord to use only a small amount of land, if any at all, for his own needs, and has become accustomed to receiving a money wage instead of depending upon a garden or field for a part of his food. He has neither farm animals, nor seed, nor implements, and he has little knowledge of how to grow food for his family. Efforts of the United States Department of Agriculture to increase the consumable crops have so far met with little success, and agricultural experts are not hopeful as to what can be accomplished.[11]

Puerto Rico's population depends largely upon outside sources for food. This dependence is to be explained in part by specialization in the growing of sugar cane. The American tariff, while affording Puerto Rico a market for its sugar, practically forces the island to buy its food and many other necessary articles from the United States.[12] Ninety-five percent of the total trade of the island is with the United States.[13] On account of high production costs, Puerto Rico is unable to compete in a world market and must sell her sugar in the United States where the price is protected by the tariff. At the same time, the tariff on foreign goods forces Puerto Rico to buy her food and manufactured articles from the United States. This being true, the Puerto Rican worker, whose annual income is only a few hundred dollars per year, has to purchase goods at American prices which may be much higher than those prevailing in the world market. So great is Puerto Rico's dependence on outside sources for food that the failure of boats to bring the regular supplies even for a few weeks would cause hardship. Rice, one of the most important articles in the diet of the poorer classes, is not grown on the island. The bulk of the beans, which with rice constitutes the principal food of a large percentage of the population, is imported. Puerto Rico cannot begin to supply its people with meat products, animal fats, milk and dairy products, and many

---

[11] DeGolia, *op. cit.*, p. 65.

[12] Tobacco and certain fruits also have tariff advantages. The annual reports of the governor of Puerto Rico include statements of the amount of imports and exports of the island. See also *Porto Rico, What It Produces and What It Buys*, U. S. Department of Commerce, *Bulletin No. 785*, 1932.

[13] Governor of Puerto Rico, *Annual Report*, 1936, p. 15.

other essential articles of food.[14] This dependence exists to a lesser degree for clothing and miscellaneous manufactured articles. Puerto Rico's present system of growing one principal money crop and exchanging it for imported food cannot easily be changed. Aside from legal difficulties connected with our present system of property rights, there are economic difficulties: on account of the island's very dense population, rich sugar-cane land which is worth several hundred dollars per acre cannot be used for the growing of beans, potatoes, or vegetables. To use it in this way for crops of lesser value would cause a great loss of income to the island.[15] Agricultural experts doubt that the arable land of Puerto Rico could feed its present population if all this land were used for the production of consumable crops.[16]

MINERAL RESOURCES AND INDUSTRIALIZATION

There are in Puerto Rico a number of different mineral resources, but practically all of them are of doubtful commercial value at the present time. The island is especially poor in those resources which would afford the basis for power. There is practically no chance that either coal or oil will be discovered on the island.[17] Copper deposits of vein origin are found on the island, but preparations to mine these deposits were never completed and

[14] The per capita imports for Puerto Rico are the highest in the entire world with the exception of Hawaii. See *Puerto Rico, Commercial and Industrial,* published by the Department of Agriculture and Commerce of Puerto Rico, Bureau of Supplies, Printing, and Transportation, San Juan, 1934, p. 3. "Few of the world's areas are so completely dependent upon external trade as Puerto Rico," says DeGolia, *op. cit.,* p. 15. See also Mixer, *op. cit.,* p. 66, and Diffie, *op. cit.,* pp. 22 and 212. This dependence upon outside sources for food is not something which has grown up entirely since the American occupation. In 1898 Puerto Rico was far from self-supporting.

[15] "With but seven-tenths of an acre [of arable land] per person, crops of low average value per acre will result in low income and a consequent lowered standard of living."—U. S. Department of Agriculture (Puerto Rico Experiment Station) *Report,* Mayaguez, Puerto Rico, 1935, p. 4. The loss of income which would result from breaking up the large farms is an extremely important point which is often neglected by economists in dealing with Puerto Rico's problem. Numerous devices, such as that of taxation, have been suggested as a means of overcoming these so-called "property rights."

[16] DeGolia, *op. cit.,* p. 66, and Clark, *op. cit.,* p. 520.

[17] H. A. Meyerhoff, *Geology of Puerto Rico,* p. 124. Also see *Report of the Committee on Mineral Resources of Puerto Rico,* Bureau of Supplies, Printing, and Transportation, San Juan, 1934.

have been abandoned. A little gold has been found, but at no time has its production been of any importance. The extraction of manganese ore constitutes the island's only substantial mining activity. There is one small mine at Juana Diaz which has been producing about 2,500 tons per year. With recent improvements, this production should be almost doubled. There is little evidence to justify the investment of money for the development of any of the metals and from a practical and commercial standpoint, mining in Puerto Rico will probably be confined to the exploitation of rock products such as limestone products and clay. The island is practically without timber resources, as all of the virgin timber has been used. Lumber is shipped from the Continent for building purposes.

Water power in Puerto Rico has already been developed. The plant in the Guayama District is probably the best example of a successful venture in procuring power from this source. The fluctuation in rainfall and the tropical floods and hurricanes make the development of water power costly. Inasmuch as the more favorable sites have already been exploited, further expenditure for water power may prove so costly that the advisability of these ventures will be questionable.

It may be said, therefore, that Puerto Rico is practically without mineral resources and that manufacturing, with the exception of the development of limited water power, would have to depend upon imported fuel. On account of the scarcity of these resources, there is no prospect that the extraction of minerals will ever be of any importance in furnishing employment to the people, or that mineral resources will ever provide a basis for extensive industrialization.[18]

At the present time, manufacturing is not extensively developed in Puerto Rico, and people who come from the island have had little experience in the important classes of industrial work found in such a city as New York. Except for a few small factories devoted to making goods for local use, Puerto Rico's industries have developed along two lines: the manufacture of products directly connected with the island's fruit and other agricultural industries; and needlework on handkerchiefs and various other articles of

[18] The 1930 census shows only 364 people engaged in the extraction of minerals.

wearing apparel.[19] The chief goods of the class first mentioned include tobacco products, canned fruits such as grapefruit and pineapple, alcohol, molasses, and a few other similar products. The second classification represents needlework and sewing on articles sent to the island from the mainland. The handwork on these articles is contracted for in Puerto Rico by agents and in a strict sense this type of enterprise represents income from the sale of labor rather than industry on the island. Other small industries not falling within either of these two classifications include the making of such articles as hats and buttons.[20]

An industry such as that of needlework offers little promise of ever being able to support the rapidly increasing population. As in the case of sugar, Puerto Rico is also dependent upon tariff protection for the sale of its needlework in the United States.[21] "Its needleworkers, poorly paid as they are, do not compete on a wage basis with those of China or the Philippines."[22]

Not only is there little manufacturing in Puerto Rico at the present time, but any program of extensive industrial development which would be large enough to relieve pressure and thus affect migration would encounter the most serious obstacles.[23] The island is practically without mineral resources; it is located in the tropics; and such things as its many destructive storms and unsettled political status could easily cause a hesitancy on the part of American and foreign investors. The apparent advantage in the use of material found on the island and low-priced labor could be entirely offset both by the factors of large-scale production on the mainland, differences in the degree of skill of workers, and force

[19] For a discussion of the industries of Puerto Rico and the possibilities of future industrial development, see Clark, *op. cit.*, Chapter XVII.

[20] In 1934 there were four hat factories in Puerto Rico. One shell-button factory near San Juan employs an average of 275 persons. The shell used by this factory has to be imported. There are also two small establishments which cut and polish jewels. See Puerto Rico, Department of Agriculture and Commerce, *Puerto Rico, Commercial and Industrial*, p. 13.

[21] The protection afforded the Puerto Rican needlework by the tariff is 90 percent ad valorem.—DeGolia, *op. cit.*, p. 31.

[22] *Ibid.*, p. 25. The wages paid in this industry are discussed on p. 36. See also Caroline Manning, *The Employment of Women in Puerto Rico*, U. S. Department of Labor (Women's Bureau), *Bulletin No. 118*, 1934, and Diffie, *op. cit.*, pp. 180-81.

[23] For a general discussion of industry and commerce as bases for the support for the population, see W. S. Thompson, *Population Problems*, Chapter VI.

of advertising, and by the practices of semi-monopoly interests seeking to retain control of the island's market. In 1930 about three-fourths of the people of Puerto Rico lived in rural areas, about forty percent of the entire population were illiterate, and a large percentage of them suffered from a chronic disease such as malaria or hookworm.[24] There is no hope of Puerto Rico's ever being able to support a dense population by industry and trade. The growth in population must slow up or the people must migrate.

PRESENT GOVERNMENT AND THE MOVEMENT FOR INDEPENDENCE

Future migration from Puerto Rico, which today is perhaps the most unhappy possession of the United States, may depend to a very large extent upon the final settlement of the political status of the island. In recent years the movement for independence which has grown up on the island has now assumed importance. If complete independence were granted there might be a restriction of immigration which would cause Puerto Ricans practically to stop coming to the United States.[25] On the other hand, if independence were granted and the present tariff protection were suddenly withdrawn, economic distress on the island might cause many Puerto Ricans to migrate to this country if they were permitted to do so.

As is well known, Puerto Rico became United States territory as a result of the Spanish-American War of 1898. The Jones Act passed by Congress in 1917 gave the island its present status as a territory, with the possibility of statehood, and made the Puerto Ricans citizens of the United States. The legislature of Puerto Rico, consisting of a senate and a house of representatives, is elected by the people. The governor of Puerto Rico is appointed by the President of the United States. The island also has a resident commissioner at Washington, who may speak in the House of Representatives but who does not have a vote. Except for the

---

[24] The population is discussed in the following chapter. See pp. 25 and 42.

[25] For example, the quota for the Philippine Islands was placed at fifty persons per year.

governor and one or two department heads, all of the political offices on the island are now held by Puerto Ricans.

Up until a sort time ago, there were three main political parties in Puerto Rico: the Liberals, the Republicans, and the Socialists.[26] While no generalization would apply to all of the members of any of these parties, the Republicans have generally been in favor of statehood and are called "pro-American." The Liberal Party, although seriously divided at the present time on many issues, have implied in one way or another that they stood for some sort of autonomous government or for independence. Socialist leaders have declared themselves strongly in favor of continued relations with the United States and for statehood, but whether this feeling is shared generally by the mass of the workers is questionable. Regardless of political party, the anti-American feeling is a dominant and growing force throughout the island today.

In addition to the three major political parties named above, a small Nationalist Party has existed for many years.[27] Pedro Albizu-Campos became the leader of this party in 1930 and declared himself to be the "President of the Republic." He was successful, by means of speeches and campaigns, in greatly increasing the strength of the movement and in making many new converts. Campos and a few of his leaders were finally tried in the summer of 1936 and convicted of sedition.[28] Almost every month since that time, either some new development in Puerto Rico's political situation or a sensational court trail has kept the island in a continued state of excitement. Puerto Ricans are coming to realize that the independence question is one which must be met in some way and settled before very long.

The importance of the independence movement and the possibility of a change in the political status of the island which would affect migration is shown not only by the Nationalist agitation on

[26] A survey of the development of the political parties is given by Enamorado-Cuesta, *op. cit.*, Chapter XIII.
[27] Diffie, *op. cit.*, presents a valuable survey of the material dealing with the growth of the anti-American feeling on the island. Chapter IX, *passim*.
[28] A good account of this movement which ended in the assassination of Col. Francis E. Riggs is given in *Time*, March 23, 1936.

the island but also by Washington's reaction to this movement. Many have interpreted statements made by officials of the Administration to mean that the Administration is entirely willing to consider independence for the island.[29] In April of 1936, Senator Tydings, then Chairman of the Insular Affairs Committee, introduced in the Senate a bill, commonly known in Puerto Rico as the Tydings Bill, to grant independence to Puerto Rico.[30] This proposal was very similar to the Tydings-McDuffie Bill which gave independence to the Philippines.

The economic penalties imposed by this bill would have brought financial collapse to Puerto Rico. Among other things, it proposed to limit immigration from Puerto Rico to the United States to 500 persons per year. It was denounced by all of the political leaders on the island, and parades and agitation broke out again.The recent trouble on the island, in which about ten people were killed and more than fifty were wounded when the police attempted to break up a Nationalist parade, has brought no revival of such proposals as that made by Senator Tydings, and today the independence question remains as unsettled as ever.[31] The final disposition of this issue will be one of the most important factors determining future migration from the island.

[29] *Ibid*. See also an article in the magazine section of the New York *Times* of Sept. 30, 1936, entitled "The Outposts of Our Empire," by Dr. Ernest Gruening, who was at that time Director of Territories and Island Possessions.

[30] The number of this bill was S 4529. See *U. S. Congressional Record,* Senate Vol. 80, Part 6, April 23, 1936, pp. 5925-27. It will be noted that this record shows that at the time the bill was being proposed Senator Tydings stated that it would be submitted with the approval of the Administration, presumably meaning President Roosevelt.

[31] The New York *Times* of March 22, 1937, gives an account of what the Puerto Ricans call the "Massacre" which occurred at Ponce on Palm Sunday.

CHAPTER III

Composition, Growth, and Economic Conditions of the Population of Puerto Rico

THIS chapter will first take up the population which is dependent upon the resources discussed in Chapter II. The pressure of population upon resources is obviously an important factor in causing the poor economic conditions which are next described. These facts about the economic and social conditions in Puerto Rico are important in the study of the migration because they shape the mode of life on the island, condition the migrant before he leaves, and are the impelling forces behind the movement. The voluntary limitation of the birth rate and migration away from the island will be briefly discussed as two possible alternatives available to the Puerto Rican people in attempting to solve their problem.

THE POPULATION

COMPOSITION

The migrant from Puerto Rico is the result of an intermixture of Spanish, Indian, and African cultural elements which has been going on since the island was first settled. Although some traces of Indian features may still be seen, the native Indian tribes on the island were quickly absorbed by the invading Spaniards. The mixture with Negro blood started with the importation of slaves and has continued down to the present time. The fusion of the three main elements is so complete that in many cases it is impossible to tell which one predominates. It is also difficult in many instances to know whether or not a person is entirely without Negro blood. Professor Rosario, in writing about the characteristics of the Puerto Rican people, says:[1]

[1] Quoted from Clark, *op. cit.*, p. 546.

Racial statistics in Puerto Rico are only approximations to the truth, as the population is extremely intermixed, and there are not only two colors, but an infinity of shades. It is next to impossible, in many cases, to determine whether a person is white or slightly colored. In such cases, of which there are thousands, the strictness or tolerance of the census agent determines how the person is to be classified.

In spite of this intermixture, it should not be inferred that there are no people of pure Spanish blood on the island. Many pure white strains have always existed, and are, in fact, the dominating influence in Puerto Rico today. It is not uncommon to hear the entire Puerto Rican people referred to in the United States as colored. Misstatements of this character are deeply resented by the white Puerto Ricans.

The census classification shows that Puerto Rico's population is predominantly white. Only about twenty-five percent, according to the 1930 census, were colored. The number in "other races" is so small that it is of no importance:[2]

White	1,146,719	74.3%
Colored	397,156	25.7%
Other races	38	

Inasmuch as color in Puerto Rico is in so many cases a matter of degree, there are probably important differences in the basis for classifying individuals according to color for census purposes in Puerto Rico and in the United States. A study of the changes taking place in the intercensal periods indicates that intermixture is going on at a rapid rate and that within a comparatively short time the people of pure Negro blood will be practically non-existent.[3]

The colored Puerto Rican usually finds much less discrimination on the island than in the United States. This difference in attitude is quite important for the colored migrant. Although there is plenty of evidence to show that color is important in Puerto Rico, there appears to be little actual discrimination in business, and even in the professions, against people who have colored blood.

[2] *U. S. Census of 1930, Outlying Territories and Possessions*, Table 2, p. 136.
[3] Fred K. Fleagle, *Social Problems in Porto Rico*, p. 2.

PUERTO RICO STILL LARGELY RURAL

In the country from which the Puerto Rican migrant comes, a little less than three-fourths of the people live in rural areas. A comparison of the census of 1935 with the two preceding ones shows a movement of the population from the rural sections to the towns and cities. This movement was greatly accelerated in the decade from 1920 to 1930 and in the period from 1930 to 1935.

Table 3. URBAN AND RURAL POPULATION OF PUERTO RICO: 1935, 1930, AND 1920[a]

Population	1935 (Dec. 1)	1930 (Apr. 1)	1920 (Jan. 1)
Urban	512,020	427,221	292,841
Percent of total	29.7	27.7	22.5
Rural	1,211,514	1,116,692	1,006,968
Percent of total	70.3	72.3	77.5
Total	1,723,534	1,543,913	1,299,809

Source: *Census of Puerto Rico, 1935*, "Population" (Number and Distribution of Inhabitants), *Bulletin No. 1*.

[a] This census was taken by the Puerto Rican Reconstruction Administration, under the immediate direction of an official from the Bureau of the Census in Washington, and was printed by the U. S. Government Printing Office. See p. 1.

"Urban population of Puerto Rico, as defined by the Census Bureau is, in general, that residing in cities and towns or urban places having 2,500 inhabitants or more, the remainder being classified as rural."—*Fifteenth Census of the U. S.* (1930), *Outlying Territories and Possessions*, p. 133.

No large number of people may be expected to come directly from the mass now living in the isolated rural areas of Puerto Rico. A word about the condition of the average rural worker will show why this is true. The literature about Puerto Rico is filled with descriptions of the wretched condition of the *jíbaro*.[4] Before the time of the large American-owned plantation, he lived in a sort of feudal state and depended upon the large planter. In many instances, he owned a few acres of land. As the population of the island grew and a large part of the land was sold to the sugar interests, it became more difficult for him to remain in his former home. Many of these workers drifted into the cities and towns; others clung tenaciously to the land. A large percentage of these

[4] Clark, *op. cit.*, Appendix A, pp. 537-75; Fleagle, *op. cit.*, Chapter II.

rural workers now live on land owned by their employers. In many cases, the *jíbaro* owns his house but not the land on which it stands. Some rent homes in the cities and towns and work on a farm nearby. In the rural sections and far away from any towns, one is seldom out of sight of a little hut or cabin which the *jíbaro* has made for himself in some out-of-the-way place. Inside the small hut, there is little which might be called furniture except a few boxes, a table, and some hammocks. The cooking utensils consist of a pot and a few homemade dishes. The *jíbaro* invariably has a large family. There may also be several relatives living with his family in the crowded hut. A scarcity of food always exists for the large number of hungry mouths. Not always is he able to provide rice, beans, codfish, and vegetables in sufficient quantities. Occasionally, depending upon the work available, he may have pork, milk, or flour. After a cup or two of black coffee for breakfast, he may walk several miles to his work, and work until dusk for less than a dollar. All of his family may go barefoot. He often suffers from malaria, hookworm, or other chronic diseases. His knowledge of the outside world may not extend farther than that gained from a trip to a nearby town. For these reasons, as will be pointed out later, the movement of people from the island is not directly from rural areas, but is by way of the towns and cities.

OCCUPATIONS

The agricultural background of the Puerto Rican migrant is clearly shown by an examination of the types of industry in which the workers of Puerto Rico are employed. In 1930, the census enumeration disclosed that there were 503,805 Puerto Ricans over ten years of age who were gainfully employed. More than one-half of these were employed in agriculture.

The poverty of Puerto Rico is apparent from the fact that about ten percent of its total number of workers are employed in domestic and personal service. About nine percent of the total number of workers are engaged in "Independent Hand Trades" which include needlework and home sewing. Over seventy percent of the entire number of those gainfully employed worked in agriculture, on needlework or some other small hand trade, or in domestic and personal service. The number of workers employed in the types of industry found in large American cities is small.

Two-thirds of all of the male workers of Puerto Rico are employed in agriculture. Of the total of 250,651 classified as doing agricultural work, 201,981 were farm laborers, 40,726 were

Table 4. GAINFULLY OCCUPIED WORKERS IN PUERTO RICO IN 1930, BY IMPORTANT OCCUPATIONAL CLASSIFICATIONS

Industry	Total Number	Percent of Total	Male	Percent Total Male	Female	Percent Total Female
Agriculture	262,623	52.1	250,651	66.3	11,972	9.5
Domestic and personal service	48,243	9.6	11,187	3.0	37,056	29.5
Independent hand trades	44,903	8.9	3,105	.8	41,798	33.2
Wholesale and retail trades	37,144	7.4	34,907	9.2	2,237	1.9
Transportation	17,137	3.4	16,522	4.4	615	.5
Mfg. food and allied products	15,606	3.1	15,042	4.0	564	.4
Cigar and tobacco factories	15,508	3.1	6,055	1.6	9,453	7.5
Building	12,760	2.5	12,683	3.3	77	—
Professional service	12,311	2.4	5,966	1.6	6,345	5.0
Other and unclassified	37,570	7.5	21,885	5.8	15,685	12.5
Total	503,805	100.0	378,003	100.0	125,802	100.0

Source: *Fifteenth Census of the U. S.* (1930), *Outlying Territories and Possessions*, Table 26, p. 170.

farmers (owners and tenants), and the remainder were foremen, managers, or had some miscellaneous farm occupation.[5] This means that over eighty percent of all of these male agricultural workers were farm laborers. The agricultural worker of Puerto Rico is not, therefore, usually a farm operator or a farmer, but a landless worker who is dependent upon a daily wage. About two-thirds of all of the women workers are engaged in personal or domestic service, or depend upon some hand trade such as needlework. Such figures emphasize the poverty of the average family in Puerto Rico.

From the data given, it may be generally observed that the Puerto Rican worker is, in most cases, unskilled, and his background is primarily agricultural rather than industrial.

[5] The source of these figures is the same as that for Table 4.

PUERTO RICO A COUNTRY WITH A LARGE PROPORTION OF CHILDREN

The large proportion of children found in Puerto Rico not only indicates that a rapid growth in population is taking place, but is also important because of its effect upon the standard of living. There is a heavy burden of support because of this condition. Table 5 shows that in 1930 forty-two percent of the entire population of the island were under fifteen years of age, while the United States had less than thirty percent in this age group.

Table 5. THE AGE COMPOSITION OF THE POPULATION OF PUERTO RICO AND THE UNITED STATES IN 1930

Age Period (Years)	Puerto Rico	Percent	United States	Percent
All ages	1,543,913	100.0	122,775,046	100.0
Under 5	226,468	14.7	11,444,390	9.3
5 to 14	423,359	27.4	24,612,486	20.0
15 to 24	335,486	21.7	22,422,493	18.3
25 to 44	359,393	23.3	36,152,869	29.4
45 to 64	159,581	10.3	21,414,981	17.5
65 and older	39,404	2.6	6,633,805	5.4
Age unknown	222	—	94,022	0.1

Source: *U. S. Census, 1930, Outlying Territories and Possessions*, p. 136, Table 3, and Vol. III, Part I, p. 36, Table 44.

In Table 5 the number of children under five years of age in 1930 is shown to be 226,468. In 1920, the number under five years was 200,255.[6] These figures show that there was an increase of 26,213, or about thirteen percent, in the number of children in this age group during this ten-year period. In 1930 the number of children under five years of age per 1,000 women of child-bearing age, or from fifteen to forty-five years, in Puerto Rico was 638 and in the United States was 391.[7]

GROWTH

The rate of population growth now taking place in Puerto Rico is the most important single fact about the migration. It is to be

---

[6] *Fourteenth Census of the U. S.* (1920), *Outlying Territories and Possessions*, p. 137. During this period there was a decline in the number of children in this age group in the United States. See Vol. III, Table 3, of the 1920 *Census*, which discloses that there were 11,573,230 children under five years of age in 1920 as compared with 11,444,390 in 1930, as shown by Table 5.

[7] *U. S. Census, 1930.* Since 1930 the number in the United States has declined to an even lower figure.

expected that migration during the next decade or two will be greatly accelerated because of a terrific increase in the number of people on the island. As the Puerto Rican can come to the United States without legal restriction, this growth may mean that many thousands will seek relief from the poverty and poor living conditions of the island by moving to this country.[8]

Table 6 shows the growth in the population of Puerto Rico from 1765 to 1935.

Table 6. POPULATION OF PUERTO RICO, 1765 TO 1935

Year	Population	Increase over Preceding Census		Intercensal Period	
		Number	Percent	Years	Months
1935 (Dec. 1)	1,723,534	179,621	11.6	5	8
1930 (Apr. 1)	1,543,913	244,104	18.8	10	3
1920 (Jan. 1)	1,299,809	181,797	16.3	9	8½
1910 (Apr. 15)	1,118,012	164,769	17.3	10	5⅙
1899 (Nov. 10)	953,243	154,678	19.4	12	
1887[a]	798,565	66,917	9.1	10	
1877	731,648	148,340	25.4	17	
1860	583,308	135,394	30.2	14	
1846	447,914	117,863	35.7	14	
1832	330,051	109,159	49.4	17	
1815	220,892	65,466	42.1	15	
1800	155,426	85,176	121.2	25	
1775	70,250	25,367	56.5	10	
1765	44,883	—	—	—	

Source: *Census of Puerto Rico, 1935*, p. 1.
[a] Month and day of censuses prior to 1899 are not given in the census reports.

During a period of about thirty-six years from the time of the census of 1899, or from about one year after the American occupation, to December 1, 1935, the population of Puerto Rico increased more than eighty percent. For the approximate period of thirty years prior to 1930, the increase per decade was approximately eighteen percent. In the period from the census of 1930 to the census of 1935, however, a period of five and two-thirds years, there was an increase in number of over eleven and one-half percent. This fact shows that a rapid and increasing rate of growth

---

[8] The ease of movement, the low cost of passage, and the various ways by which the Puerto Rican manages to get to the United States will be discussed in Chapter IV. This statement is not intended to convey the impression that all of Puerto Rico's people will be able to migrate.

is taking place at the present time. The actual increase in the number of persons during the last period of a little less than six years is greater than in the period from 1899 to 1910, and is practically the same as the increase in number from 1910 to 1920. The data

Table 7. ANNUAL RATE OF POPULATION GROWTH IN PUERTO RICO IN SELECTED PERIODS, 1877–1935[a]

Period	Years	Months	Rate of Growth Percent—per Year
1877 to 1887	10	0	.88
1887 to 1899	12	0	1.48
1899 to 1910	10	5⅙	1.54
1910 to 1920	9	8½	1.56
1920 to 1930	10	3	1.69
1930 to 1935	5	8	1.95

Source: *Census of Puerto Rico, 1935*, p. 1.

[a] A discussion of the geometric mean to measure population growth and a useful formula for its calculation will be found in R. E. Chaddock, *Principles and Methods of Statistics*, pp. 126-27.

in Table 7, above, show that the rate of growth has increased during each period since the island became a part of the United States, and that the rate of growth of 1.95 percent per year during the last period, ending in 1935, is more than one-fourth greater than the period in which the American occupation took place.[9]

NATURAL INCREASE BY GROWING EXCESS OF BIRTHS

The explanation of this astounding rate of population growth, which may soon cause an increased migration from the island, is to be found in the high birth rate and the declining death rate. Puerto Rico at the present time has one of the highest birth rates in the civilized world. The birth rate of Puerto Rico in 1935 was more than twice as high as that of the United States, and the excess of births over deaths was more than three times as great per 1,000 of the population:[10]

[9] This figure of 1.95 percent for each year represents an extremely high rate of population growth. A population growing at the rate of 1.75 percent per year will double itself in about forty years. At the rate of two percent per year, it would double in approximately thirty-five years.

[10] Commissioner of Health of Puerto Rico, *Annual Report*, 1935-36, pp. 11, 58; Bureau of Census, *Vital Statistics*, Jan., 1937, Vol. III, No. 1.

Country	Birth Rate (per 1,000)	Death Rate (per 1,000)	Excess of Births over Deaths
Puerto Rico	40.4	18.4	22.0
United States	16.9	10.9	6.0

Since the time of the American occupation, the published birth rates have shown an increase; and the published death rates, a decrease. The changes in these rates are brought out by the following comparison:[11]

	Birth Rate (per 1,000)	Death Rate (per 1,000)
Five-year average 1900-1904	29.0	26.4
Five-year average 1931-35	40.3	20.6
Increase (decrease)	11.3	(5.8)

These figures show an increase in the birth rate of nearly forty percent, and a decrease in the death rate of twenty-two percent. A large part of the apparent increase in the birth rate results from the incompleteness of registration in the earlier years. It is well known that in the years immediately following the American occupation the registration of births was defective. For instance, in 1911 the governor of Puerto Rico stated in his annual report that it could be safely estimated that one-eighth of the births which occurred on the island were not registered.[12] Because of this incompleteness of registration the actual increase in population which may be ascribed to changes in the birth and death rates cannot be determined, but there has been a large natural increase caused by the growing excess of births over deaths.

DENSITY

Another fact which clearly suggests that an increased movement of people from the island will take place is the mounting population density. Although, as has been previously indicated, Puerto Rico has few resources to support a rapid growth in numbers, it has already reached the status of one of the most densely populated

---

[11] A comparison of the birth and death rates from 1900-04 to 1925-28 will be found in Clark, "Porto Rico and Its Problems," *op. cit.*, p. xxiv. The figures for the period from 1931 to 1935 have been taken from the reports of the Commissioner of Health.

[12] Page 261.

areas in the entire world.[13] The average number of persons per square mile in Puerto Rico is twelve times that of the United States. Although Puerto Rico, an agricultural country, should not be compared with countries of Europe which are, for the most part, industrialized, it is rapidly approaching, and in some cases already exceeding, the population density of these countries. Table 8 shows the figures of reported population density of Puerto Rico as compared with selected countries.

Table 8. POPULATION DENSITY OF PUERTO RICO COMPARED WITH THAT OF OTHER COUNTRIES[a]

Country	Population Density per Square Mile
Java	822
Belgium	694
Netherlands	641
Puerto Rico	507
British Isles	491
Japan	446
Germany	351
Italy	349
Cuba	90
Dominican Republic	62
Hawaii	59
United States	42

[a] The figure for Puerto Rico is that given in the bulletin of the Bureau of the Census, *Population of Puerto Rico, 1935*, p. 1. The figure for the United States is based on the population estimated by the Census Bureau for 1934, 126,626,000, and an area of 2,973,776 square miles. See Bureau of the Census publication, *Mortality Statistics, 1934*, p. 3. Other population densities in the table have been taken from the *Report of Puerto Rico Experiment Station, 1935*. These figures were for the years 1934 and 1935. The reader will of course appreciate the difficulty of arriving at correct population densities and especially of obtaining comparable figures. The data given are intended to be indicative only and will serve the purpose intended at this point.

The rapid increase in the population density of Puerto Rico is brought out by a comparison of the present figure of 506.8 per square mile with figures of the previous census years. In 1899, soon after the American occupation, the number of people per square mile was only 280.3. In the period from the census of 1930

[13] "The *effective* density of population in Puerto Rico is perhaps the greatest in the world."—Earl P. Hanson, "The Dilemma of Puerto Rico," *Science and Society*, Vol. I, No. 4 (Summer, 1937), p. 501.

to the latest census, 1935, a period of a little less than six years, the density per square mile increased from 454.0 to the present figure of 506.8. The density per square mile for the various census years is as follows:[14]

1899	280.3
1910	328.8
1920	382.2
1930	454.0
1935	506.8

If it were possible for the present rate of growth to continue, it would not be many years before Puerto Rico would reach a population density equal to that of Java at the present time. The rate of growth, as shown by Table 7, was 1.95 percent per year for the period from 1930 to 1935, and 1.69 percent for each year in the decade from 1920 to 1930. If we should take an arbitrary figure between these two rates, 1.8 percent per year, and assume that Puerto Rico's rate of growth would continue at this rate, the population and density per square mile would increase as follows:

Year	Population	Density per Square Mile
1940	1,884,000	554
1950	2,252,000	662
1960	2,692,000	792

The length of time during which the present rate of increase can continue is problematical. If Puerto Rico has to depend entirely upon its own resources, and nothing is done to check the present rate of birth, disease and starvation will slow the rate of increase. On the other hand, migration, while not by any means a final solution to the problem of a crowded country, might relieve population pressure temporarily.

ECONOMIC AND LIVING CONDITIONS

WAGES

The poor standard of living of the migrant before he leaves the island becomes apparent from an examination of wages paid in

[14] *Census of Puerto Rico, 1935.* The Bureau computes density on the basis of 3,400.6 square miles.

Puerto Rico. The great difference between wages in the island and in a city such as New York is an important factor in causing migration; it also suggests problems which might arise from a large and continuing migration of these poorly paid workers to Northern industrial centers.

Table 9. COMPARISON OF WAGES IN PUERTO RICO AND CONTINENTAL UNITED STATES

Industry	Average Earnings per Hour		Average Full-time Weekly Earnings	
	P.R.	U.S.	P.R.	U.S.
Bakery shops				
Males	$.147	$.553	$ 9.26	$30.42
Females	.187	.298	9.00	14.93
Males and females	.147	.548	9.26	30.09
Cigarette factories				
Males	.345	.378	15.56	18.86
Females	.189	.268	6.76	13.37
Males and females	.272	.318	10.90	15.87
Foundry, machine, and blacksmith shops				
Males	.16	.601	8.43	30.23
Men's clothing				
Males and females	.145	.701	5.70	31.05
Women's underwear				
Males	.199	.408	7.96	20.85
Females	.123	.260	4.92	13.16
Males and females	.127	.292	5.08	14.80
Slaughterhouses				
Males	.167	.470	6.73	23.12

Source: *Report* of Commissioner of Labor of Puerto Rico, 1934-35, p. 42.

The money wage paid in Puerto Rico is, in most cases, only a fraction of that paid for similar work in the United States. In spite of this fact, it is often said that the laborer in Puerto Rico buys imported food at the same price as the American worker, or at possibly a slightly higher price.[15] Some relief from this situation is afforded by the use of the cheaper native foods, the fact that a tropical climate demands less expensive housing and clothing, and the practice of purchasing cheaper grades of merchandise. A com-

[15] Data to support this statement are given in Diffie, *op. cit.*, pp. 177-79. Retail prices of food in Puerto Rico are also given in the *Report* of the Commissioner of Labor of Puerto Rico, 1934-35, p. 60.

parison of wages paid in Puerto Rico with those paid in the United States is shown in Table 9.[16]

In a survey made by the Department of Labor of Puerto Rico, in the fiscal year 1934-35, of the wages of 70,395 workers, it was found that the most common rate of wages was between twelve and thirteen cents per hour.[17] Some of the industries surveyed paid as low as five cents an hour for men and four cents an hour for

Table 10. AVERAGE EARNINGS PER WEEK OF WORKERS IN PUERTO RICO IN THE FISCAL YEAR 1933–34

Industry	Average Earnings per Week	
	Men	Women
Transportation	$10.15	$
Manufacturing children's garments	9.66	3.18
Sugar manufacturing	9.04	4.71
Building trades	8.59	
Manufacture of cigars	8.49	5.16
Manufacture of hats	8.49	6.01
Ladies' underwear	6.89	3.02
Miscellaneous	5.55	3.38
Manufacture of furniture	5.53	
Tobacco stripping	5.39	2.98
Planting of sugar cane	4.44	2.99
Wharf and allied industries	4.20	
Fruit planting	2.93	.70
Coffee planting	2.12	1.61
Cultivation of tobacco	2.10	1.53
Fruit packing	1.68	1.13

Source: *Bulletin No. 6* of the Department of Labor of Puerto Rico, by A. P. Rodrigues, 1935: *A Report Dealing with Labor Statistics, Cost of Living, Housing Conditions, and Craftsmanship of Workers in Puerto Rico for the Fiscal Year, 1933-34*, p. 28.

women workers. A little more than fifty-four percent of the 70,395 workers received wages of ten cents or less per hour, and only about one percent received more than forty cents per hour. In terms of weekly wages, this means that more than fifty percent of these workers earned about five dollars per week. Examples of

[16] It is realized that this comparison is limited. The *Report* of the Commissioner of Labor of Puerto Rico states (p. 41): "The table following shows such comparison with bakery shops, cigarette factories . . . [and other industries given in Table 9], the only ones of our industries for which recent data will be found in the bulletins of the United States Bureau of Labor Statistics." Sources of the wages for the United States are indicated in this report. The years covered were from 1930 to 1932.

[17] Commissioner of Labor of Puerto Rico, *Annual Report*, 1934-35, pp. 40-41.

average weekly earnings for various industries are given in Table 10. The range is from one to ten dollars.

The Department of Labor of Puerto Rico estimated the number of individuals in a family of average size to be five, and the average monthly rental to be seven dollars. The actual cost of food to feed a family of this size properly in 1933-34 was calculated to be about seventy-five dollars per month.[18] A minimum subsistence level for a family at that time required about thirty dollars per month.[19] Wages such as those given in Table 10 show that the worker must spend practically his entire income for food, and even then he lives in a half-starved condition.

The extremely low wages in the factories and in agriculture are, however, far in excess of the earnings of the home sewers and needleworkers. In the winter of 1933-34, a survey of 323 workers of this class revealed that the hourly earnings "for 31.4 percent of the women were less than one cent; for 31.1 percent, they were one and under two cents; and for 31.4 percent, they were two and under four cents."[20] In other words, about ninety-five percent earned less than four cents per hour. The home worker doing needlework often does well to earn ten cents per day.[21] In this industry there are more than 44,000 workers, or about nine percent of the total number of gainfully occupied workers living on the island.

Domestic servants form an important group, numerically, of the total workers. The actual money received by them, in addition to food and shelter, may be only a few dollars per month.

The deplorable condition of the Puerto Rican worker may be easily understood after a study of these facts. If the high money wages of the United States have in the past attracted workers from Europe, it would seem that this attraction would be doubly effective in the case of the Puerto Rican, whose poverty is so extreme

---

[18] These estimates are given in the Rodriques report, *Bulletin No. 6* of the Department of Labor of Puerto Rico, 1935, p. 10.

[19] Dorothy D. Bourne, director of Social Work Training, University of Puerto Rico, "Puerto Rico's Predicament," *Survey*, Vol. LXXII, No. 7, July, 1936.

[20] U. S. Department of Labor, Woman's Bureau, *Bulletin No. 118, The Employment of Women in Puerto Rico*, p. 2.

[21] *Ibid.*, p. 20.

that it might delay his departure from the island in spite of his desire to migrate.

HOUSING

The overcrowding and unsanitary conditions likely to be encountered by any newcomer to the slum sections of our large American cities would not be new things for the Puerto Rican. Even in these substandard areas he is apt to find better conditions than those of his former home. The poor housing conditions found on the island are a natural consequence of the extremely low wages; they accompany the general low standard of living in Puerto Rico today.

The houses occupied by the skilled workers are, as would be expected, far superior to those of the average rural worker and to those of a large number of unskilled workers who have taken up their residence in the larger cities. The better-paid workers, who form only a small group, occupy apartments and houses of frame and stucco construction which compare favorably with average dwellings in the United States. On the other hand, one who has been in Puerto Rico for only a few hours must realize that the average home of the Puerto Rican worker represents miserable conditions. Slum conditions of the worst sort prevail in certain sections of the larger cities.[22] Near the outskirts of some of them, numerous shacks have been built by people of the very poorest class. In many cases the land is rented and the house is constructed from waste lumber and other materials which the family has been able to get together. It is not uncommon to see these shacks elevated on poles in very poorly drained areas, so that most of the time there is water standing under them. A large family may live crowded together in one of these little shacks. While there are probably factors of greater importance than poor housing, this is undoubtedly one cause of the poor health conditions which prevail.

An idea of the housing of the workers may be gathered from a survey made in 1933-34 by the Department of Labor of Puerto

[22] See the description in the *Report of Puerto Rican Relief Administration*, by James R. Bourne, administrator Aug. 19, 1933, to Aug. 31, 1934, published by the Bureau of Supplies, Printing, and Transportation, San Juan, 1935, pp. 17ff.

Rico.[23] Of a total number of 1,696 houses selected at random, 666 were owned and 1,030 rented. In the owned group, it was found that in most localities the houses had less than the cubic space per person required by the Department of Health of Puerto Rico.[24] The average cubic air space per person in the entire group of 666 houses was also below this requirement. In the owned houses, there was an average of 4.82 persons per dwelling; eight percent of the dwellings had baths. Only six percent had toilets; in the rest, the families used latrines. The 1,030 rented quarters were

Table 11. NUMBER OF PERSONS PER ROOM IN 4,268 RURAL HOUSES IN PUERTO RICO

Persons per Room	Number of People	Percentage of Total
Less than 1	342	1.0
1 to 2	4,805	14.7
2 to 3	7,458	22.8
3 to 4	6,833	20.9
4 to 5	5,603	17.1
5 to 6	3,176	9.7
6 to 7	1,674	5.1
7 to 8	950	2.9
8 to 9	561	1.7
1 to 10	441	1.3
10 to 11	390	1.2
11 to 12	242	0.7
12 to 13	96	0.3
13 to 14	91	0.3
14 or more	48	0.3
Total	32,710	

Source: V. S. Clark, *Porto Rico and Its Problems*, p. 20.

also found to be overcrowded. In these houses, it was calculated that there were about three persons to each bedroom. Thirty-six percent of the rented houses had baths and thirty-seven percent had toilets.

On account of the extreme poverty of the rural worker, many of the houses in the country are nothing more than huts. Yet in

[23] Rodrigues, *A Report Dealing with Labor Statistics, Cost of Living, Housing Conditions, and Craftsmanship of Workers in Puerto Rico*, pp. 9, 10. This report contains pictures of various types of houses and the rental paid.

[24] "With reference to dwellings, the Department of Health of Puerto Rico requires that the cubic space per person shall not average less than 500 cubic feet and that the average amount of pure air required per person should be 3,000 cubic feet," *ibid.*, p. 9.

these small houses, which in many instances have only one or two rooms, overcrowding is about as great as it is humanly possible for it to be. V. S. Clark made a study of 4,268 of these rural homes for the Brookings Institution report. Concerning the conditions found, he makes the following statements:[25]

A majority of the one, two, and three-room houses have more than eight people living in them. In fact, the size of the family remains about uniform, irrespective of the size of the home. More than 50 per cent of the single-room shacks house eight or more people, and in 4 per cent of the cases as many as 13 people occupy the hut. Extreme cases are reported of 16, 18, and 20 people to a one-room shack.

These crowded conditions are clearly shown by Table 11 which classifies the data found in this investigation according to the number of persons per room.[26]

HEALTH CONDITIONS ON THE ISLAND

Health conditions in the mother country have an important bearing upon migration. These conditions begin to affect the migrant in earliest childhood and may continue to affect him during his entire life in the United States. Thus, the physical quality of the entire group which migrates is to some extent determined by these health conditions. If the migrant suffers from a chronic disease which he contracted before he came to this country, he may fail to gain economic security and consequently may become dependent upon the community. Also, if there is a large movement of people these unfavorable conditions and diseases may be transferred to the community in which the people settle. There is, of course, an additional danger to the community in the case of contagious diseases.

Health conditions in Puerto Rico are such that they might easily prove detrimental to a large proportion of the people who come, or will come, from the island to the United States. These conditions are not only unsatisfactory but are in some respects alarming. This is true despite the fact that remarkable improvements have been made since the American occupation, and at the present time the appropriation for health and sanitation represents

[25] V. S. Clark, op. cit., p. 20.
[26] This survey represents conditions in the early part of 1929.

the second largest governmental expenditure. In Puerto Rico, however, a part of the benefit in welfare from the public health movement has been offset by the fact that increasing numbers have caused further pressure upon resources, tending to lower wages and standards.

The mortality rates from certain diseases, shown by Table 12, reveal the unfavorable health conditions generally found on the island.

Table 12. DEATH RATE FOR SELECTED DISEASES IN PUERTO RICO IN 1935[a]

Cause	Rate
All causes (per 1,000)	18.4
Infant mortality (per 1,000 living births)	114.7

Disease	Deaths per 100,000 of Population
Tuberculosis	304.5
Diarrhea and enteritis (under 2 years)	240.1
Pneumonia	155.5
Nephritis	133.7
Diarrhea and enteritis (2 years and over)	128.5
Malaria	126.2
Bronchitis	44.3
Syphilis	32.2
Uncinariasis (hookworm)	23.5

Source: Commissioner of Health of Puerto Rico, *Annual Report,* 1935-36, pp. 56 and 71.

[a] The mortality rate for the United States for all forms of tuberculosis in 1935 was 55.0 per 100,000. Other rates were: Diarrhea and enteritis, under two years, 10.4; Malaria, 3.5; Diarrhea and enteritis, two years and older, 3.7; Bronchitis, 3.1; and Syphilis, 9.1. (Source: Bureau of Census, *Vital Statistics,* Release April 9, 1937, Vol. III, No. 10, p. 57.)

The mortality rate for tuberculosis per 100,000 population is between five and six times that of the United States. The effect of poor sanitation, overcrowding, and poverty is shown by the very high rate of death from diarrhea and enteritis in the age group under two years. The rates for diseases such as pneumonia, bronchitis, and nephritis are also much higher than those found in this country.[27] In contrast to the United States, malaria and hookworm still rank high among the causes of death.

[27] On account of the great difference in the age groups, mortality statistics of Puerto Rico and the United States are not always comparable. For example, it might appear that Puerto Rico has a decided advantage over the United States in cancer

In Puerto Rico, tuberculosis, a disease which is extremely important from the standpoint of migration, is the outstanding health problem. In many countries the death rate from tuberculosis has been declining, but in Puerto Rico the mortality rate from this disease has increased from about 175 in the years from 1910 to 1914 to about 300 per 100,000 in the period from 1930 to 1934. Pulmonary tuberculosis is responsible for practically all of the deaths from this disease.[28] The Commissioner of Health in his report for the year 1934-35 states as follows:[29]

According to studies carried out by the Insular Department of Health, tuberculosis mortality in the island is 17 per cent higher in women than in men; 19 per cent higher in the colored than in the white race; and 84 per cent higher in the urban than in the rural districts. Approximately 68 per cent of children under fifteen react positively to the intrademic tuberculosis test, the incidence of positive reactors being 37 per cent higher in urban than in rural districts.

Among the important factors presumably responsible for the increase of tuberculosis mortality in Puerto Rico, cognizance should be given to overcrowding in urban districts as a result of the migration of families from rural areas to city slums; the lack of employment which brings overcrowding in dwellings; the relatively low economic status of the island population and the lack of hospital facilities for the isolation of tuberculosis cases.

The fact that Puerto Ricans who move to the United States are from a country where the tuberculosis mortality rates are higher than in any other country in the civilized world for which statistics are available[30] cannot help but affect both the migrant's

---

mortality. In 1934 the mortality rate per 100,000 for cancer for Puerto Rico was 47.1 compared with a rate of 111.2 for the United States. In 1934 the estimated population of the continental United States was 126,626,000. If we look at Table 5, page 28, we find that about 17.5 percent of the total population, or approximately 22,160,000 persons, were in the age group of from 45 to 64 years. *Mortality Statistics, 1934* (p. 162) shows that 59,590 persons in this age group died from cancer and other tumors in 1934, which would give a mortality rate of something like 270 per 100,000 for people of this age group. In Puerto Rico the estimated number of persons in this age group in 1934 was 168,575, and the number of deaths from this cause was 371 (Commissioner of Health, *Annual Report*, pp. 56 and 71), which would give a mortality rate of about 220 for this group. This lack of comparability also exists for diseases of the heart.

[28] *Annual Report*, 1934-35, p. 13.
[29] *Ibid.*
[30] Mandry Costa, M.D., "Epidemiology of Tuberculosis in Puerto Rico," *Puerto Rico Journal of Public Health and Tropical Medicine*, Vol. IV, July, 1928.

health in this country and the health of the community in which he settles.

Of even greater prevalence and of almost as great importance are the parasitical diseases found among the Puerto Ricans. These diseases are not only a menace to health and often a cause of death, but they are notorious for causing an incapacity for work. Investigations have disclosed that nearly ninety percent of the rural population and about forty percent of the urban population are suffering from hookworm.[31] It can be safely said that the majority of Puerto Rico's entire population is infested with one or more types of these parasites; like tuberculosis, such a health problem is extremely important where migration is taking place.

The infant mortality rate, which, like tuberculosis, is an index to living conditions, shows the possible effect of health conditions on the island upon the migrant. Puerto Rico's infant mortality rate is approximately twice that of the United States.[32] In 1934-35, diarrhea and enteritis was the leading cause of death among infants, being responsible for about thirty-five percent of all of the infant deaths. The fact that such a large percentage of the infant deaths resulted from this cause is proof of the effect of poor sanitation and poverty. The death rate among children normally is highest in the first year. In Puerto Rico, however, there is not the normal sharp decline in the death rate in the second year. This fact is said to be the result of inadequate and improper food.[33] The pasture land has been converted into large sugar-cane plantations, and milk is expensive and often contaminated. Besides, there is a scarcity of physicians and trained nurses in some districts, and in too many cases the people would be unable to pay for these services even if they were adequate.[34]

Such poor standards and such a degree of poverty as exist in

---

[31] Walter C. Earle (Rockefeller Foundation), *American Journal of Tropical Medicine*, X, 120.

[32] Commissioner of Health of Puerto Rico, *Annual Report*, 1934-35, p. 79, and *Births, Stillbirths, and Infant Mortality*, 1934, p. 3.

[33] Helen V. Bary, *Child Welfare in the Insular Possessions of the U.S.* U. S. Department of Labor, Children's Bureau Publication No. 127, 1923, p. 18.

[34] Due largely to a grant from the Puerto Rican Emergency Relief Administration, the Department of Health has been able to do remarkable work in the line of maternal care and infant hygiene. See Commissioner of Health, *Annual Report*, 1934-35, p. 42.

Puerto Rico may even affect, to some extent at least, the physical characteristics of the people who migrate. In 1923, a study of 7,362 boys and girls of from six to sixteen years of age in selected schools as to height and weight was made, and it was the opinion of those who made these measurements that parasitical diseases and poor economic conditions contributed to the fact that there was difference in height and weight in different districts on the island. Because of the various factors involved, no exact comparison can be made of these heights and weights with those of children of the same age in the United States; on the average, however, both the weight and height of Puerto Rican children tend to be lower.[35]

EDUCATION

Another problem in connection with migration from the island arises from the fact that educational standards in general are far lower in Puerto Rico than in the United States. It is hardly necessary to do more than point to the high rate of illiteracy in Puerto Rico, which in 1930 was about forty percent of the population, to make clear the difficulty encountered in the field of education.[36] Such a high proportion of people who are unable to read or write indicates that the present standards are low and that many people, though literate, have not attended more than a few years of the elementary school. This lack of school training is especially unfortunate since the Puerto Rican usually moves to a large city rather than to a rural district of the United States. He is poorly equipped to enter such a highly competitive labor market and his comparative lack of education may deprive him of all work except the lowest-paid and most menial.

Although improvements in education since the American occupation have been nothing short of remarkable, it cannot be expected that Puerto Rico will be able to educate the mass of its inhabitants within a short time. In 1899, about ninety percent of the people were illiterate; in 1930, about forty percent. It will require another long period of years to bring the literacy to a fairly high standard. Even if the additional funds and facilities could be

[35] Bary, *op. cit.*, p. 28.
[36] *U. S. Census, 1930, Outlying Territories and Possessions*, Table 7, p. 141.

provided, many people of the very poorest class would be unable to take full advantage of them. Many of the adults living in the rural districts are almost beyond the reach of any educational program. It is difficult to force people, by compulsory school laws, to go to school when many of them live under the conditions found in Puerto Rico.

The Puerto Ricans are by no means a bilingual people, and the language difficulty, or the inability to speak English at all, is of course a serious handicap for the workers who migrate. According to the census enumeration in 1930 eighty percent of the population of ten years of age and over did not speak English.[37] Notwithstanding the rather high percentage which is shown by the census figures as being able to speak English, one cannot escape the conclusion, after living in Puerto Rico, that only an extremely small percentage of the people, outside of the most highly educated class, have a sufficient command of English to make it possible for them to enter the United States without a definite language handicap.[38] Spanish is universally the language of the home and the street. It is now used as the language of instruction in the schools, and English is taught in much the same way as Spanish would be taught in the United States. In recent years the problem of teaching English, which is generally an unpopular subject with Puerto Rican students, has become increasingly difficult on account of the growing anti-American feeling. There is no specific educational movement to prepare Puerto Ricans to migrate.

ECONOMIC DISTRESS AGGRAVATED BY THE DEPRESSION

Although even before the depression there was extreme poverty in Puerto Rico and conditions were far below a satisfactory standard, the disastrous hurricane of 1932 and the prolonged depression added greatly to the suffering of the Puerto Rican people. For example, in the year 1927 the annual average per capita income of Puerto Rico was estimated to be $111, as compared with $738 for the continental United States.[39] In 1932,

[37] *Ibid.*, Table 9, p. 143.
[38] "As a rule the Puerto Ricans are sadly deficient in the knowledge of English."
—Governor of Puerto Rico, *Annual Report*, 1936, p. 10.
[39] Clark, *op. cit.*, p. 202.

when there was general unemployment and business conditions approached one of the lowest levels of the entire depression, the island was visited by one of the most destructive storms in its history.[40] The distress of the people seemed to culminate with this event. Large programs of relief were necessary to prevent actual starvation.[41] Improvement in these conditions since the worst periods of the depression has not been particularly encouraging. As late as 1936, a large proportion of the entire population of the island was dependent upon public relief measures of some kind. In July of 1936 it was stated that "eighty percent of Puerto Rico's population has been, and is, eligible for relief."[42] The situation was described at that time as "appalling," with many facing want and starvation. Dr. Ernest Gruening, director of the Division of Territories and Island Possessions of the United States, in an article written in September of 1936, dealing with attempts of the government to solve the economic problems of the island possessions and territories, stated that eighty-two percent of the total population were on relief rolls and that the government's rehabilitation and relief program was only a beginning if Puerto Rico's needs were to be cared for.[43]

The terrible suffering and poverty which the Puerto Rican people have endured during the past few years may have an important bearing on migration. As will be shown in later chapters, no actual net movement of people to the United States took place during the worst period of the depression. Beginning in 1934, migration was resumed. To what extent the cessation of relief for a large proportion of the people on the island will affect migration can be told only by the figures for later years.

[40] For details of the effect of the hurricane of 1932, see *Annual Report of the Governor*, 1933, pp. 1-6 and Appendix A.

[41] Under the most favorable conditions only about 65 percent of Puerto Rico's working population (that is, the people who would be defined as gainfully employed by the census enumeration) are employed. In 1933, only about 35 percent of these people were employed.—*Report of the Puerto Rican Emergency Relief Association*, 1935, p. 7. A summary of conditions before the advent of the Relief Administration is given on p. 17 of this report. See also Diffie, *op. cit.*, pp. 166 and 167

[42] Bourne, "Puerto Rico's Predicament," *Survey*, July, 1936.

[43] "The Outposts of Our Empire," New York *Times*, Magazine Section, September 30, 1936. Dr. Gruening wrote the author that the figure of 82 percent was supplied by the Federal Emergency Relief Administration which was in charge of this problem in Puerto Rico from 1934 until 1936.

PRESSURE OF POPULATION UPON RESOURCES AND ITS CONSEQUENCES

Estimates have been made which show that Puerto Rico cannot adequately support more than about 1,000,000 people through agriculture.[44] It has few available land or mineral resources, and there is little in the way of industrial development. It is also dependent, for the most part, upon outside sources for food. In spite of this fact, a terrific growth in population is taking place. In each census period since the American occupation the rate of growth has been higher than in the previous period. The apparently increasing birth rate now stands at about forty per 1,000 persons. On the other hand, the death rate is being lowered. Puerto Rico has thus quickly become one of the most densely populated areas of the world.

Puerto Ricans who talk of the days when the peasant had land and when food and shelter were comparatively easy to obtain are apt to attribute the increasing difficulties of the island entirely to political injustices and exploitation and fail to consider the ever-increasing strain which population puts on the island's resources.[45] V. S. Clark, in the Brookings Institution report, published in 1930, summarizes what is taking place in Puerto Rico in the following statement:[46]

> The reason why Porto Rico's population has increased more than twice as fast as that of the British islands may be found in the relatively rapid economic development. These figures compel us to conclude that under existing conditions the population multiplies to the subsistence limit as determined by the relatively low living standard of the tropics. In this respect, Porto Rico is repeating the history of Java and Japan. Human reproduction keeps step with physical production.

There is little doubt that the rapid economic development of the island would not have taken place had it not been for the invest-

---

[44] *Report of the Puerto Rican Emergency Relief Association,* p. 7.

[45] The question of whether the present system of land concentration and its attendant evils have been forced on the Puerto Rican people is highly controversial. Every legislature, representing at one time or another each of the major political parties, has refrained from enacting legislation which would make the "500-acre law" effective.

[46] Page XXV. It is to be noted that this statement was made in 1930, prior to the tremendous increase in growth of the latest period. See table showing rate of growth, on p. 30.

ment of American capital. Despite the fact that the advantages from this development have been offset by the very nature of the economic system under which the island operates, the fundamental problem of the island is the pressure of population upon resources and the working out of some plan to take care of, or to check, its future growth in numbers.

Economic conditions found in Pureto Rico clearly show the effect of population pressure. The low wages and chronic unemployment which have existed for years are natural consequences of this pressure. The home which the average worker can provide with his meager wage is usually poor, lacks sanitary conveniences, and is too small for his family. Extremely crowded conditions are found in practically all of the rural homes. The consequences of low wages, inadequate food, poor housing, and unsanitary conditions are reflected in the health of the inhabitants. Year by year, the alarming mortality rate from tuberculosis, which is almost six times that of the United States, increases. The high infant mortality rate clearly points to crowded conditions, poverty, and bad sanitation. The growth in population has been far too rapid to be taken care of by means of rehabilitation programs. With more than three-fourths of the total population dependent upon governmental relief of one form or another, there has grown up an intense general dissatisfaction with conditions in Puerto Rico. The Puerto Rican people must solve their problem by a voluntary limitation of population growth by means of birth control, or they must send large numbers away from the island to escape its poverty, disease, and lack of opportunity. These are the two principal alternatives of the Puerto Rican people.

TWO MAIN ALTERNATIVES FOR RELIEVING POPULATION PRESSURE

THE OUTLOOK FOR BIRTH CONTROL

There is little chance that the severe pressure of population in Puerto Rico will be relieved through a voluntary limitation of births. In fact, there is practically the opposite trend, and the population is growing at a more rapid rate than ever before. The factors involved in a question of birth control are, of course, numerous, and are so intimately connected with the life of the people as to make an analysis difficult. For example, it is evident that religion might have an important bearing on a question of this kind. We do know that the majority of the Puerto Rican people are Catholic, and the Church will continue to oppose the practice of any form of birth control by its members. In 1932, Governor Beverly pointed to overpopulation as the chief problem of the island and said that new solutions were necessary to the population problem in addition to the alleviation brought about by the organization of agriculture and the encouragement of new industries.[47] This statement was interpreted to mean that he favored birth control, and therefore met with the strongest sort of protest from the Church and other organizations.[48] The Church contends that not birth control but the regulation of marriage is needed and that the cause of the unsatisfactory social conditions is the many illegal and consensual marriages existing among the people. Yet in Puerto Rico the influence of religion on the question of birth control might be less than in some other countries because in Puerto Rico there is less strict adherence, especially on the part of men and young people, to the rules of the Church. Consensual relations are in themselves evidence of a disregard for these rules. Although religion is a factor of importance, it is probable that if Puerto Rico had the same incentives and standards of living as other countries, its birth rate would decline as it has in other Catholic countries.

At the present time, of course, the practice of birth control is not prevalent in Puerto Rico. Although the dissemination of birth-control information has been advocated by a few of the educated leaders for many years, the effect of the movement today is of little consequence. Recently, certain social work directed toward birth control was started on the island. This work was done through medical clinics and in connection with a health program. In spite of the facts that contraceptive information was furnished only to mothers who, from the standpoint of health, should not have additional children, and that the majority of these mothers

[47] Governor of Puerto Rico, *Annual Report*, 1932, pp. 7 and 8.
[48] In his report for 1933 (p. 7), Governor Beverly withdrew somewhat from his former position, and said: "There has been some acrimonious discussion in and out of Puerto Rico as regards the population question and its economic results, and the question of birth control. In this report, only the statistics are presented, from which any person may draw such conclusion as he sees fit."

had several children already, the movement met with the strongest opposition from the Church and a few of the island's political leaders.

The difficulty in the path of the birth-control movement in Puerto Rico lies mainly in the low standard of living of the people. People who rigorously limit the size of their families are usually striving to attain a higher standard of living or to maintain a certain relatively high standard. Puerto Rico is tropical and largely rural. The majority of the people lack entirely the incentives which cause many of the middle class in the United States, for example, to have small families. A subsistence level in Puerto Rico is far below that of the temperate zones. Sexual development takes place at an early age. Extramarital relations in Puerto Rico very often result in the birth of children. The high rate of illegitimacy and the large number of homeless children testify as to the nature of sexual relations among a large percentage of the population.[49] Any voluntary limitation of the birth rate to the extent that it exists in such a country as the United States is so unlikely to take place in the near future that it merits little consideration. It will be extremely difficult to secure improved standards of living so long as the population in Puerto Rico increases at its present rate; yet it appears that little could be accomplished along birth-control lines without materially improving the standard of living for the majority of the people. The difficulty of remedying a given situation in Puerto Rico is illustrated in health conditions. We know, for example, that with proper precautions, including the wearing of shoes, hookworm could be practically eliminated; yet this disease is still one of major importance in Puerto Rico. Under such conditions, how much more difficult would be the successful operation of any program of birth control. In the near future, at least, no hope can be placed in a movement for birth control in Puerto Rico as a means of solving the population problem of the island.

MIGRATION AS AN ALTERNATIVE

While migration will not prove a final and lasting solution to the population problem of a country such as Puerto Rico, there are strong indications that it will be more effective as a solution

---

[49] Bary, *op. cit.*, Part I, pp. 54-64.

than any voluntary program of birth control. Migration does relieve pressure, and may provide an escape for many from conditions found in Puerto Rico today.[50] A movement from the island to the United States has been going on for a long time, as will be shown by figures in the next chapter. Nearly every year a large number leave their homes on the island to take up life in other places, principally New York City. This migration, however, is not keeping pace with population growth. The density per square mile increased, in the period of a little less than six years from 1930 to 1935, from about 450 per square mile to over 500 per square mile. As population mounts and pressure on the island increases, relief must be found through a much larger migration than has already taken place.

So long as the Puerto Rican is free to enter the United States without restriction, it is to be expected that almost all of the migration from the island will be to this country. The main difficulty in their settling in the other islands of the West Indies is their inability to compete with the native people. Jamaica and Haiti, largely inhabited by Negroes, together with several other small but densely populated countries, can furnish workers who are better able to stand the hardships of tropical labor and who will work for even lower wages than the Puerto Ricans. Wages are considerably lower in many of the neighboring countries than in Puerto Rico. These countries are fighting the same conditions of poverty and poor standards of living that exist in Puerto Rico. Cuba has now a plan under consideration to deport many thousand foreign workers, mainly Haitians and Jamaicans of the laboring class, in order to make jobs for her own people. Puerto Ricans do not want to move to a country such as the Dominican Republic on account of the fear of political oppression. Negotiations during past years have always shown the difficulty of finding among the neighboring countries one which would accept large numbers of Puerto Ricans from the lower economic classes.

For these reasons the movement to the United States will be the important one. To this phase of the problem, we now turn.

[50] The *Annual Report* of the governor of Puerto Rico, 1936 (p. 10), suggests that a well-planned migration might relieve the pressure of population.

CHAPTER IV

The Movement of the Puerto Rican to the United States

MOTIVES FOR MIGRATION

IN VIEW of conditions described in the preceding chapter the motivating force of the high money wages reported to be paid in the United States is easily understood. As with other recent migration to the industrial East, the basis for the movement was laid during the shortage of labor at the time of the World War and during the prosperous period which came before the depression. The story of the Puerto Rican is much the same as that of other groups of people who have taken part in these movements.

Practically all reports which reach the worker in Puerto Rico emphasize the great difference in wealth, wages, and opportunity. He observes that the average American in Puerto Rico has a much higher standard of living than the average Puerto Rican. He often exaggerates the position and income of an American teacher, government employee, or business representative. American moving pictures also give him, in many cases, a distorted idea of the luxury of the American family. So strongly is this idea of the wealth of the American people fixed in the mind of the uneducated Puerto Rican that it is difficult to make him believe that the United States also has, and has always had, a large group of very poor people.[1]

Relatives and friends already in the United States exert a strong influence. Almost everyone has some friend or relative, or has known someone, who has gone to the United States and secured employment. During the prosperous period of the decade 1920-30, these friends and relatives were writing letters back to Puerto Rico or revisiting the island and telling of their life in New York. It is not difficult to imagine the effect of a letter from a girl in

[1] Information obtained from personal conversations with people in Puerto Rico.

New York to her sister in San Juan, who is receiving practically no money wages at all, telling her that she has secured a position as a domestic worker which pays her sixty or seventy dollars a month.[2] It would be expected that many of these letters would tend to exaggerate the success of the migrant who has just come to New York. People of the lower economic class in Puerto Rico seem anxious to have an American confirm the reports they have had of high wages and opportunities to be found here. Many of them think that if they, too, could get to a place where they might earn four or five dollars a day, all of their poverty and distress would be at an end. As might be expected, little consideration is given to the amount of goods this money would buy in New York, or to the many additional requirements of the climate and general living in a large city.

Many Puerto Ricans come to the United States to join relatives who are already here. As soon as persons who are here can provide passage, one by one the others come. Often the family in Puerto Rico is broken by the migration, and the cost of the trip for the first member who comes may be met in part by selling most of the household goods or other belongings of the family. In the more prosperous years, it was easier for a woman than for a man from Puerto Rico to secure work here. A married woman might leave her family and come to New York where she could live with friends until she secured work, at which time she would send for her husband. Later, arrangements would be made for friends who were coming to bring the children. Finally, the father, mother, and sister of the wife or husband might come and live with the family. Since, according to all of the social workers and others who are in close contact with the group in New York, it is customary for Puerto Ricans to share whatever they have with relatives who have just arrived and also to help other relatives to migrate, this method of migration may continue almost indefinitely.

EASE OF MOVEMENT

Because the movement of the Puerto Rican to the United States is technically one of internal migration, there are no legal restric-

---

[2] For an interesting study of the influence of letters from relatives and friends as affecting migration, see C. V. Kiser, *Sea Island to City*.

tions against his coming to the United States. Although the Department of Immigration does collect certain data as to the age, sex, and address of the migrant and the Department of Agriculture enforces regulations prohibiting the bringing of certain plants and fruits into the United States, on the whole the Puerto Rican is subject to very little inspection or regulation, and may enter this country almost as freely as a citizen of one state may move to another.

SIZE AND YEAR OF MOVEMENT

Since there is no separate classification in the census covering the Puerto Rican people in the United States, we can only judge the total number of people of Puerto Rican origin by the number born in Puerto Rico and living in the continental United States. Although the data given in Table 13[3] afford a good basis for estimate, they do not show the total number of Puerto Ricans who were living in the United States at any particular date.

Table 13. NUMBER OF PERSONS BORN IN PUERTO RICO AND LIVING IN THE CONTINENTAL UNITED STATES AT CENSUS DATES AND IN 1935

Year	Number	Increase
1910	1,513	
1920	11,811	10,298
1930	52,774	40,963
1935[a]	58,200	5,426

[a] Estimate, Dec. 31.

In order to know the total number of persons of Puerto Rican origin residing in the United States, we should add to the number given in this table the number of people born of Puerto Rican parentage but not born in Puerto Rico. There is no basis for an estimate of the number of persons who might fall into this class. We do know, however, that in places such as New York a large number of Puerto Rican children have been born. The actual number of people of Puerto Rican origin living in the United

---

[3] Sources: *1910 Census,* I, 234; for 1920 see "State of Birth of the Native Population" (a reprint of Chapter V, Vol. II), p. 630; for 1930, "State of Birth of the Native Population" (reprint of Chapter IV, Vol. II), p. 27. The Department of Labor has advised the author that there was an excess of 8,142 arrivals over departures from Puerto Rico in the period from the date of the 1930 census to Dec. 31, 1935; it is their estimate that two-thirds are Puerto Ricans (letter from Edward J. Shaughnessy, Deputy Commissioner, Sept. 9, 1936).

States at this time must, therefore, be placed at a considerably higher number than the estimate of 58,200 persons.

It will be observed from Table 13 that the major part of the movement of the Puerto Rican people took place in the decade 1920-30. If the estimate given for the end of the year 1935 is substantially correct, the 58,200 persons living in the United States in 1935 and born in Puerto Rico resulted from the excess of arrivals over departures in the following periods: 2.6 percent before 1910; 17.7 percent, 1910-20; 70.4 percent, 1920-30; and 9.3 percent, April, 1930, to December 31, 1935.

Table 14. MOVEMENT OF U. S. CITIZENS BETWEEN PUERTO RICO AND THE CONTINENTAL UNITED STATES, 1921-35

Fiscal Year	Arrivals from Puerto Rico	Departures to Puerto Rico	Excess of: Arrivals	Departures
1921	9,480	7,694	1,786	
1922	6,576	7,059		483
1923	9,036	6,829	2,207	
1924	11,512	7,231	4,281	
1925	11,279	8,136	3,143	
1926	14,455	9,212	5,243	
1927	19,161	9,728	9,433	
1928	17,034	10,808	6,226	
1929	15,911	9,462	6,449	
1930	18,617	9,290	9,327	
1931	11,517	12,625		1,108
1932	9,683	10,385		702
1933	8,700	9,953		1,253
1934	11,569	7,466	4,103	
1935	13,174	10,214	2,960	
Total	187,704	136,092	55,158	3,546

Source: Figures supplied by U. S. Department of Labor.

One important point to keep in mind in considering the migration of the Puerto Rican people to the United States is that the settlement of a few thousand persons in this country is the net result of a very much larger movement of people to and from the island. Table 14 gives the movement of citizens between Puerto Rico and the continental United States for the fiscal years from 1921 to 1935.

It is to be understood that by no means all of the travelers shown in Table 14 are Puerto Ricans; but the years in which the movement of people from the island has taken place are, however, clearly indicated. The movement began soon after recovery from the depression of 1921 and continued throughout the years up to 1930. During the worst years of the depression, there was a net movement back to Puerto Rico. Beginning with the year 1934, there is again an excess of immigration to the United States. The relation of economic conditions to the movement is clearly shown by these facts. It appears that in the period from the time of the census of 1930 to the end of 1935 about 6,000 Puerto Ricans settled in the United States. During this period there was a movement back and forth of many times this number. This is accounted for by the unusual economic conditions prevailing in the United States during most of this period. Many Puerto Ricans found conditions so bad that they desired to return to their former homes. Relief also had a part in the unusual movement of people which took place. Puerto Ricans, like citizens of other states, were often returned to the island.

PLACES OF SETTLEMENT

It might seem at first glance that the logical place for the settlement of the Puerto Rican worker in the United States would be in the rural and agricultural sections of the South. Florida, Louisiana, and certain parts of Texas have a climate which is not radically different from that of Puerto Rico. Florida is nearer to Puerto Rico than is New York. These localities are similar to Puerto Rico in that they are not highly industrialized, and some of them even have the same industries as the island, such as sugar and fruit.

The advantages which these localities might have for the Puerto Rican are discovered to be only apparent, however, when the situation is more carefully examined. With the number of trained Negroes already at a low standard of living in the South, there is good reason for the feeling on the part of the Puerto Rican that this section of the country is a place of small opportunity. In addition to this feeling, there is the fear of racial discrimination which might be encountered. Also, there is plenty of Cuban as well as native colored labor in Florida. Texas and California are already supplied with Mexican labor in the sections where there would be a climatic advantage for the Puerto Rican. California also has its Oriental workers and people from the Philippine Islands employed at relatively low wages. In addition to these facts, consideration must also be given to the fact that during the years in which a large part of the migration took place, 1922-30, it was the urban centers which were unusually prosperous, and not the rural areas of the South or West. The attraction of high money wages comes from cities and not from farming sections.

Another reason for the migration of the Puerto Rican to New York rather than to other sections may be found in the better transportation facilities from Puerto Rico to New York as compared with those to the Gulf and other Southern ports. The most important trade routes are between San Juan and New York, rather than between San Juan and Tampa, Galveston, or New Orleans. Some of the steamship lines which operate between San Juan and the Gulf ports provide only first-class passage for a limited number of passengers. The cost of passage is, as a rule, much higher to any of these Gulf ports than to New York. Between San Juan and New York, there are several boats each week which bring large lists of passengers. On the faster boats the traveling time is only about three and one-half days. Cabin-class boats require from four to five days. The lowest cost of passage is forty dollars. Men frequently secure passage by working on the boats, but there appears to be no evidence to show that the movement of people from Puerto Rico has been artificially stimulated by the granting of lower rates by the steamship company to groups of Puerto Ricans who were migrating to this country.

Another important factor is that when once a settlement is started and becomes as large as the Puerto Rican settlement in New York, there is a sort of pull from it to people on the island. People planning to migrate want to join relatives and friends in New York and to be with people of their own racial group rather than to go to some isolated rural place in Texas or Florida. Added to this is the attraction found in the very size of New York. It is the city about which Puerto Ricans know most, from which many of their supplies come, and in which there are already many of their countrymen.

Data of actual places of settlement in this country show a strong tendency for the Puerto Rican to move to the North and East. The places of residence of the 52,774 persons born in Puerto Rico

Table 15. PERSONS BORN IN PUERTO RICO AND LIVING IN THE CONTINENTAL UNITED STATES, BY GEOGRAPHICAL DIVISIONS AND STATES, 1930 AND 1920

Divisions and States	1930		1920	
United States total		52,774		11,811
Middle Atlantic		47,528		8,512
New York	45,973		7,719	
New Jersey	947		360	
Pennsylvania	608		433	
Pacific		1,862		984
California	1,795		935	
Others	67		49	
South Atlantic		1,012		878
Florida	252		200	
Maryland	250		127	
District of Columbia	185		148	
Virginia	143		163	
Others	182		240	
East North Central		737		414
Illinois	252		142	
Michigan	230		98	
Ohio	188		124	
Others	67		50	
West South Central		515		317
Texas	324		84	
Louisiana	169		217	
Others	22		16	
New England		477		274
Massachusetts	263		163	
Connecticut	158		69	
Others	56		42	
Mountain		380		90
Arizona	292		31	
Others	88		59	
West North Central (each state less than 100)		147		160
East South Central (each state less than 100)		116		182

Source: U. S. Census.

and living in the continental United States in 1930 are shown by Table 15. It will be observed from this table that while in 1930 ninety percent of this number lived in the Middle Atlantic states, in 1920 only seventy-two percent of them lived there. Practically all of the Puerto Ricans who came to the United States in the period between 1920 and 1930 settled in the Middle Atlantic states, principally New York. Between 1920 and 1930 there was a total increase of 40,963 in the number of Puerto Ricans living in the United States, and of this total number 39,016 settled in the Middle Atlantic states; of the latter number, 38,254 settled in New York State. These figures show an increase of 458 percent in the number of persons born in Puerto Rico and living in the Middle Atlantic states in 1930, as compared with an increase of 496 percent in the number of persons born in Puerto Rico and living in New York State.[4]

There has not only been a tendency for Puerto Ricans to settle in the industrial East, but also a very marked tendency for them to settle in New York City. This fact is clearly brought out by a comparison of the number of persons born in Puerto Rico and living in New York City at different times:[5]

Date	Number	Increase
1920 (Census)	7,364	
1930 (Census)	44,908	37,544
Dec. 31, 1935 (Estimate)	49,500	4,592

Of the total of 45,973 persons who were born in Puerto Rico and who lived in New York State in the year 1930, only 1,065 lived outside of New York City. The movement of people has been to New York City, and not to New York State. The group living in the metropolitan area, including those who lived across the Hudson River in the state of New Jersey and in other sections outside the limits of the city, would without doubt include almost ninety

---

[4] Of the total number of people living in New York State in 1930 who were born in other states of the Union, there were larger numbers from only eight states than from Puerto Rico. This is an interesting fact when we consider the densely populated adjoining states, and also when we consider that the migration of the Puerto Rican people took place for the most part in the decade from 1920 to 1930. See bulletin of the Census Bureau, *State of Birth of the Native Population*, 1930, Table 21, pp. 23 ff.

[5] The figure for 1920 may be found in the bulletin of the Census Bureau, *State of Birth of the Native Population*, 1920, Table 25, p. 679. The figure for 1930 is not given in a similar report for the 1930 census and has been taken from a report of the Health Department of New York City, by John L. Rice, "Health Problems among Puerto Ricans in New York City," 1934 (unpublished), p. 1. The estimated figure of 49,500 has been calculated by taking 85 percent (the percentage of the total number living in New York City in 1930) of the total estimated to have come to the United States since 1930, which was 5,400, and adding this to the number given in the census for 1930. See p. 53 n.

percent of the people born in Puerto Rico and living in the United States in 1930. The facts about the place of settlement of approximately 53,000 Puerto Ricans living in the United States in 1930 may be summarized by saying that about ninety percent of the settlement was in the Middle Atlantic states; about eighty-seven percent, in New York State; about eighty-five percent, in New York City; and approximately ninety percent, in the metropolitan area of New York City.

IMMEDIATE ADJUSTMENTS FOR THE PUERTO RICAN MIGRANT
WHO MOVES TO NEW YORK

The fact that the Puerto Rican migrates to New York rather than to a place more like his native environment suggests the adjustments which he is forced to undergo. During a major part of the year, the difference in climate alone would call for an important adjustment. Linen suits are worn throughout the year in San Juan, and there is no need for heating devices of any kind. In spite of this, one sometimes hears people in Puerto Rico speak of the "cool weather" of such a month as January. Even during the summer months, in case of a cool spell of weather in New York, there would be danger of "colds" for the person coming from Puerto Rico. This adjustment may be, in part, mental. Even as a fear of the tropics exists among people of temperate zones, the cold of the northern climate is feared by the untraveled and uneducated class of tropical countries.

Perhaps the adjustment to a great urban environment such as that of New York City is as trying on the people from Puerto Rico as any other adjustment which they must make. It is probably much greater than that required by the immigrant from one of the large cities of northern Europe. As a Puerto Rican of the poorer economic class, clad in heavy clothing and wearing an overcoat for the first time, lands at the foot of Wall Street, the city with its dark and smoky skies, its elevated and subway lines, and its tall buildings must create a feeling not soon to be erased from his memory. This would be true even though the migrant came from San Juan, the largest city in Puerto Rico, with a population of well over one hundred thousand, but not a complicated industrial center. Its narrow streets often appear to be as densely crowded as places in New York, and the noise seems fully as great at times as that of New York, except for the elevated-railway sections. San Juan's buildings, however, are small; the methods of transportation are simple; and a person may walk over most of the entire business section of the city in a short time.

These adjustments to climate and urban environment are only a few of the many which the migrant must make in his new home. He will soon face, also, the severe competition of a new labor market, discrimination, and problems of housing and relations with new racial groups. Some of these adjustments will be discussed in later chapters which deal with the worker and his family after they have taken up residence in New York.

SEX AND COLOR OF THE MIGRANTS

In the migration from Puerto Rico to New York City, the percentage of males is only slightly higher than that of females. In 1930 the figures were as follows:[6]

	Number			Percent	
Total	Male	Female		Male	Female
44,908	23,947	20,961		53.3	46.7

The equality of numbers between the sexes as shown by these figures might be taken to indicate that the Puerto Rican migration is almost entirely a family movement. There are no statistics available on this question, but information secured from social workers in New York indicates that in many cases either the husband or the wife has remained in Puerto Rico, and that many single people of each sex have migrated to this country.

Of the total of 52,774 persons who were born in Puerto Rico and were residing in the United States in 1930, 11,132, or about twenty-one percent, were colored.[7] In 1930, approximately twenty-six percent of the population were classified as "colored" in Puerto

[6] In the published reports, the census does not classify the people who were born in Puerto Rico and were living in the United States in 1930 as to sex. Since 85 percent of these people lived in New York City, these figures may be taken as a good index of the total United States. The source of the data given is Rice, *op. cit.*, p. 1.

[7] U. S. Census, *State of Birth of the Native Population*, 1930, Table 23, p. 37.

Rico.[8] In other words, there is a slight tendency for the migration to the United States to contain a greater percentage of white people than is found on the island.

SOCIAL CLASSES REPRESENTED

Although there are no published data which give specific information about the social classes represented in the migration from Puerto Rico to the United States, there is clear evidence that a large majority of the people who have come are from the lower economic classes. Any very large movement of people from the island would necessarily include many poor people. Puerto Rico's few wealthy individuals can, of course, move to the United States or to Europe as they see fit, and a few of them have done so. There is little reason, however, for their leaving successful business enterprises to move to New York. The same would be true of the professional classes. The highly educated Puerto Rican has, in past years, found an excellent opportunity in the great expansion and development of education and institutional work which has come about on the island since the American occupation. As in the United States, some fields, such as that of law, are crowded. There is still a demand in the field of medicine, and in specialized lines of engineering, which has not been met. Since educational standards are yet low in Puerto Rico, for many years to come the average teacher will have a better opportunity on the island than in the United States.

Poverty and lack of opportunity on the island cause mainly the poorer economic class living in the cities and towns to migrate. One clear proof of this fact is the place of settlement of the Puerto Rican people in New York City: about seventy percent of all of the people who have moved to New York City have settled in the Harlem and Navy Yard districts. Information in later chapters, dealing with the worker and his family in New York, bears out the fact that many of the Puerto Ricans in New York have a very low economic status. Some of these individuals, before leaving Puerto Rico, were trades people or factory workers, or

[8] See p. 24.

followed some mechanical trade. Domestic workers and servants constitute another important class. Many needleworkers and persons engaged in home sewing have also migrated. All evidence points to the fact that the average migrant, as might be expected, is of a low economic status.

Migration from Puerto Rico comes by way of the towns and cities and not directly from rural areas. As long as the *jíbaro* lives in his present isolated environment, he will not be able to attempt a trip to New York City. It is difficult for anyone to imagine this half-starved worker leaving the fields to begin a four-day ocean trip to New York. As has already been pointed out, however, many of these people will not remain in their present environment. A large number have already moved to towns and cities which will soon prepare them to migrate.

Unless brought to this country by relatives, many people of the very poorest economic class in Puerto Rico cannot migrate. Their great poverty would prevent many people now living in slums such as are found in San Juan from securing passage to New York, no matter how much they might desire to come.

THE CONCENTRATION OF THE PUERTO RICAN IN CERTAIN AREAS OF NEW YORK CITY

There is a strong tendency for Puerto Rican migration to concentrate in certain areas of New York City. As is shown in Table 16, about ninety-five percent of the total number of Puerto Ricans in New York City in 1930 lived in the boroughs of Manhattan and Brooklyn. Seventy-seven percent of this total number lived in Manhattan. It will also be noted from Table 16 that the proportion of white and colored persons from Puerto Rico in New York is about the same as that of the total Puerto Rican migration to the United States; that is, about seventy-nine percent white and twenty-one percent colored. Outside of Manhattan and Brooklyn, the proportion of white Puerto Ricans is much greater than in these boroughs. There is also a tendency for the colored Puerto Rican to settle in Brooklyn. Nearly one-third of the Puerto Rican people living in this borough are colored.

The concentration in certain areas in New York will be seen from an examination of the census data for the various statistical areas of the city.[9] In 1930, about seventy percent of the total number of Puerto Ricans living in New York City were in the four statistical areas of M-8c and M-6c in Manhattan and K-1 and K-3 in Brooklyn.[10] (See Table 17.) Puerto Ricans in New York are concentrated in two areas. Of these, the Harlem settlement is much more important. In Manhattan, Puerto Ricans

Table 16. PERSONS BORN IN PUERTO RICO AND LIVING IN NEW YORK CITY, BY BOROUGHS AND COLOR, 1930

Borough	Number White	Number Colored and Other Races	Total	Percent of City Total	Percent Borough Total White	Percent Borough Total Colored and Other Races
Manhattan	27,255	7,460	34,715	77.3	78.5	21.5
Brooklyn	5,446	2,539	7,985	17.8	68.2	31.8
Bronx	1,190	83	1,273	2.8	93.5	6.5
Queens	696	49	745	1.6	93.4	6.6
Richmond	169	21	190	.5	89.0	11.0
Total	34,756	10,152	44,908	100.0		

Source: Rice, "Health Problems among the Puerto Ricans in New York City," p. 1.

live in a district bounded by a line from about 97th Street up to and along 110 Street around the northern part of Central Park, northward to about 125th Street, and approximately from about Third Avenue on the east, to Eighth and Manhattan Avenues on the West. In Brooklyn, they are most numerous along the water

[9] The statistical area, a unit used by the Bureau of the Census, contains numerous census tracts.

[10] The boundaries of these statistical areas are as follows:
Manhattan:
M-8c W. 130th St., Lenox Ave., W. 126th St., Park Ave., E. 112th St., 5th Ave., W. 110th St., Cathedral Parkway, 8th Ave.
M-6c Cathedral Parkway, W. 110th St., 5th Ave., E. 112th St., 3d Ave., E. 109th St., East River, E. 99th St., 3d Ave., E. 98th St., 5th Ave., W. 84th St. extended, E. line reservoir, W. 86th St. extended, Central Park West.
Brooklyn:
K-1 East River, Navy Yard Basin, West line U. S. Navy Yard, Navy, Flushing Ave., N. Portland Ave., S. Portland Ave., Atlantic Ave., Flatbush Ave., 4th Ave., Bergen, Court, Atlantic Ave., Upper Bay.
K-3 Atlantic Ave. Court, Nevins, Carroll, Gowanus Canal, Gowanus Bay, Upper Bay, Buttermilk Channel.

front from the Navy Yard south to Gowanus Canal, and extending inland to about Third Avenue. There are other smaller settlements north of 125th Street in Manhattan, in the Bronx, and in the Greenpoint section. The areas of settlement are taken up in more detail in Part Two.

Table 17. NUMBER OF PERSONS BORN IN PUERTO RICO AND LIVING IN NEW YORK CITY IN 1930, BY IMPORTANT STATISTICAL AREAS

Area	Number	Percent of Total in: Borough	Percent of Total in: Entire City
New York City	44,908		
Manhattan	34,715		
M-8c	19,223	55.4	42.8
M-6c	6,895	19.9	15.4
Both M-8c and M-6c	26,118	75.3	58.2
M-5b	1,310		
M-8a	1,270		
M-7	1,264		
M-3a	1,052		
M-6b	606		
M-9a	532		
Others (less than 500 each)	2,563		
Brooklyn	7,985		
K-1	3,133	39.2	7.0
K-3	2,471	31.0	5.5
Both K-1 and K-3	5,604	70.2	12.5
Others (less than 500 each)	2,381		
Bronx, Queens, and Richmond	2,208		

From unpublished data of the U. S. census of 1930.

Puerto Ricans are the largest Spanish-speaking group in New York City. In addition to them, there are large groups from other islands of the West Indies and from Central and South America who speak Spanish. Although not all of the people from the Caribbean area speak Spanish, the size of the entire group of Spanish-speaking people in New York City in 1930 is indicated by the following figures:[11]

[11] The source of the number of Puerto Ricans has been given on p. 58. For the number born in Cuba and other West Indian islands, see Table 22, p. 116. The figure of 14,268 has been arrived at by substracting 13,032, the number of white persons born in Cuba and other West Indian islands, from the total number of white persons shown by the census of 1930 to have been born in the West Indies and in Central and South America. See *U. S. Census,* 1930. III, 297 and 301. No data is available as to the number of colored persons born in Central or South America. There is in New York a small number of Filipinos, who also speak Spanish.

Place of Birth	Number
Cuba and Other Islands of the West Indies	61,295
Puerto Rico	44,908
Central and South America (white only)	14,268
Spain	13,992
Mexico	2,152
Total	136,615

In 1930, there were also 19,371 native white persons of foreign or mixed parentage who had at least one parent born either in Spain, Central or South America, or the West Indies. The total Spanish-speaking population of New York City is probably around 175,000, of which the Puerto Ricans are the largest single group.

In conclusion it may be said that, considering the United States as a whole, the Puerto Rican migration is unimportant in size. With a total population measured in millions, the actual number coming from Puerto Rico is relatively insignificant. This number creates important problems, however, when the settlement is made principally in the largest city, and particularly when it is made in certain sections of that city.

Part Two

The Puerto Rican Worker and His Family in New York

CHAPTER V

Occupations and Employment Opportunities

IN PART ONE the conditioning and preparation of the worker for life in New York City has been discussed and the migration of a large group has been traced to the Harlem and Navy Yard sections. Part Two takes up the worker and his family after they have moved to New York. This discussion of the migrant in New York will be limited almost entirely to the families of the low-income group which have moved to the Harlem settlement.

The difficulty of sources of material for a study of this nature was stressed in the opening chapter. One reason for this difficulty is the fact that when the Puerto Rican lands in New York City he becomes lost in a great confusion of people from all parts of the world. There is no separate classification for him in the mass of statistical material of employment offices, health center districts, or welfare organizations. A few of the larger charity organizations do have case records and a few studies and reports dealing specifically with the Puerto Rican migrant. In 1930, the Puerto Rican Community Committee, made up of representatives of various social organizations, under the auspices of the Welfare Council, brought together people from many organizations who contributed mimeographed reports about the group. Several years ago a large religious institution, in the preparation of a confidential report for its own workers, interviewed more than one hundred people, and made contact with practically every institution dealing directly with the Spanish-speaking people in New York. As already stated, information such as that mentioned above has been supplemented by recent first-hand interviews. Employers, employment agencies, recreational centers, students, nurses, and religious workers have all furnished information about the group.

In this study of the migrant in New York, the employment and

70   Occupations and Employment

economic status of the worker are logically the first things to be considered. More than upon any other single thing, his success here will depend upon whether or not he is able to earn the high money wages which he has learned about on the island. The amount of money which he is able to earn will determine the character of his home, the kind of food and clothing, the medical care, the amount and kind of recreation which he will be able to obtain, and also numerous other factors which will affect his well-being and that of his family.

WHERE AND HOW THE MIGRANT FINDS WORK

Although there is no published study which deals specifically with the wages, degree of skill, and occupations of the Puerto Rican worker in New York, the background of a large number of these workers, already described, suggests the kinds of occupations which they might be able to follow here. Data in Chapter III show the low scale of wages prevailing on the island. It has also been pointed out that among the gainfully employed workers of Puerto Rico, the three most important groups consist of persons employed in agriculture, domestic and personal service, and independent hand trades. The number of persons employed in these three classifications constitute seventy percent of the total number of workers on the island. Two-thirds of the male workers are engaged in agricultural work, and two-thirds of the women workers are employed in domestic service or in some form of needlework or hand sewing. A glance at Table 4 on page 27 will show that a migration of any size would exhaust the supply of workers in many of the trades and manufacturing groups in Puerto Rico. A large number of people have, therefore, come from Puerto Rico whose former work was either connected with agriculture, domestic service, or some hand trade such as needlework.

It is important to note that the Puerto Rican is one of the most recent newcomers in the New York labor market. Many immigrants in former years, just after they arrived, did unskilled work and menial tasks. Along with the migration of the Puerto Rican, there has been an influx of other people from the West Indies and also of Negroes from the South. All of these workers have come to New York as a result of the demand for labor during the prosperous decade from 1920 to 1930. They have for the most part come to do the work which was formerly done by the newly arrived European immigrant.

There is, of course, a small professional group of Puerto Ricans in New York, made up of physicians, dentists, teachers, and others; and another group engaged in various lines of trade. No separation can be made of the Puerto Ricans in these groups from other Spanish-speaking people. Some interesting information about the entire Spanish-speaking people in New York may be obtained from their commercial directories which have been published from time to time. In one of these directories, published in 1933, there are listed about thirty lawyers, thirty dentists, more than fifty physicians, and a few other professional people.[1] Of course, not all of these people are Puerto Ricans, and not all of the Spanish-speaking professional people are listed. The information given in this directory would indicate that the grocery business is a favorite one among Spanish-speaking people in New York, as about one hundred and seventy stores selling groceries are listed. There are more than forty drug stores, about forty restaurants, thirty meat markets, and thirty-five tailors. Many grocery stores and barber shops in the Harlem section are owned by Puerto Ricans. Puerto Rican cigar stores and restaurants are frequently found in the neighborhood of Lower Harlem, where a large number of Spanish-speaking people live. The postal service in New York is reported to have a number of Puerto Ricans employed in its various departments. Practically all of the regular lines of trade are represented in one way or another. There seems, however, to be no very large business or institution, giving service to a large part of the city, owned or operated by Puerto Ricans.

The number of Puerto Ricans in the professional class and engaged in some kind of business or trade is very small. These are the more fortunate members of the group. Most of the Puerto Ricans in New York have to depend upon finding employment which will pay them a weekly wage. The greatest variety exists in the positions obtained by these workers. One is apt to find a

[1] *Guía hispana*, Guía Hispana Publishing Co., New York, 1933.

Puerto Rican in some form of building service, acting as a waiter, working in a laundry, or employed in a factory.

Even in the prosperous years before the depression, employment was one of the major problems, if not the major one, of the Puerto Rican in New York. Because of the great demand for labor, however, in earlier years before the depression, the majority of the workers from the island found it comparatively easy to secure work of some sort. The two largest employers of Puerto Rican labor in New York were a large biscuit company and a pencil factory. Puerto Ricans have always been found in laundry work. Before the depression, the salary of the worker was usually small. Some men were working for as little as ten or twelve dollars per week, and women and girls were earning in some instances as low as six or eight dollars per week. In one investigation in 1925, it was concluded that the average wage of the group of Spanish-speaking workers, including Puerto Ricans, in New York City was around twenty-one dollars per week.[2] Before 1930, unemployment was common among the group. There were at that time few agencies which took an interest in the problem of the Puerto Rican worker. He was allowed to drift, and did not, in many instances, know where and how to find work. In practically all cases he was forced to take the first job that was offered to him. The depression greatly complicated his problem. Some of the racial groups who gave up their jobs to the Puerto Rican have now come back to reclaim their former jobs.

In recent years, many Puerto Ricans, especially those who are unskilled, have secured employment from a governmental agency. In order to assist the Puerto Rican worker in New York, in July of 1930 the Department of Labor of Puerto Rico established an employment service in New York. This office is now located at 1770 Madison Avenue in the center of the Puerto Rican settlement in Lower Harlem, and is, of course, restricted to Puerto Ricans. From the time the service was instituted until the end of the fiscal year on June 30, 1936, a period of a little less than six years, about 16,500 persons had registered at the agency and more than 5,600

---

[2] The Catholic Charities, "Study of the Spanish-speaking People of the Archdiocese of New York," 1925 (unpublished), pp. 50-52.

Occupations and Employment

had found work as a result of its efforts. During the first four years of its operation, this service placed more than 1,000 workers each year. During the fiscal year 1934-35 only 718 were placed and in the year 1935-36 the number was only 574. Of the total number of approximately 5,600 workers placed in positions, about 2,000 have been men and 3,600, women. The placement for men and women by years is as follows:[3]

Year	Total	Men	Women
1930-31	1,070	200	870
1931-32	1,097	323	774
1932-33	1,028	307	721
1933-34	1,131	633	498
1934-35	718	274	444
1935-36	574	240	334
Total	5,618	1,977	3,641

The decline in the number of women placed by the service was caused by the fact that a smaller number obtained employment in needlework and domestic service in the later years. In 1930-31, the service placed 338 domestics and 245 needleworkers; while in 1935-36 it placed only 192 domestics and nine needleworkers. Despite the decline in these two occupations, it is still easier for the agency to place women than men. It is also to be noted that notwithstanding the improvement in general business conditions which took place in the later years, and the large number of Puerto Ricans then living here, the actual number of placements declined. J. M. Vivaldi, who is in charge of this agency, offers an explanation of this decline in the following statement:[4]

> During the fiscal year just ended (1934-35), this Employment Service has experienced great difficulties placing Puerto Ricans to work in this city. Employers are increasingly demanding higher standards in the quality and type of employees. Unfortunately, the majority of applicants appealing to this office for employment do not compare favorably with the requirements in demand and which are easily obtained among the great mass of unemployed at the present time.

It is also significant that in the report of the employment service for 1935-36 it is stated that the salaries paid in the occupations in

---

[3] The information given above will be found in the *Annual Reports of the Commissioner* of Labor of Puerto Rico, fiscal years 1930-31 to 1935-36 inclusive.

[4] *Annual Report,* Commissioner of Labor, 1934-35, p. 32.

which a majority of the Puerto Rican people could be employed were below the levels of the WPA and Home Relief Bureau.[5]

The data given in Table 18 show that most of the positions were for unskilled labor[6]

Table 18. PLACEMENT OF PUERTO RICANS BY THE PUERTO RICAN EMPLOYMENT SERVICE, 1930–36

Men		Women	
Occupation	Number	Occupation	Number
Laborers and construction workers	402	Domestic	1,537
Laundry workers	321	Needleworkers and hand sewers	699
Factory work (paper, leather, etc.)	238	Garment workers	694
Porters, errand boys, and domestics	157	Miscellaneous factory and machine workers	229
Hotel workers	126		
Janitors, handymen, watchmen, etc.	110	Laundry workers	171
Carpenters, painters, plumbers, and helpers	109	Stenographers, typists, office helpers	142
		Waitresses and counter girls	38
Tailors, garment workers, etc.	75	Packers	23
Office, clerical, and professional	57	Salesladies and other store helpers	20
Cooks and kitchen workers	54	Cooks, kitchen workers, etc.	12
Mfg., cigars and cigarettes	53	Hat workers, millinery, etc.	9
Auto mechanics, garage workers, and chauffeurs	44	Office cleaners, janitresses, and chambermaids	8
Salesmen and canvassers	42	Nurses and helpers	6
Clerks, grocery and drug stores	28	Miscellaneous and unclassified	53
Barbers and institutional workers	22	Total	3,641
Waiters and countermen	13		
Electric workers and other mechanical trades	12		
Pressmen (printing)	11		
Farm hands	11		
Shoemakers	8		
Bakers and butchers	7		
Shipping and packing clerks	4		
Miscellaneous and unclassified	73		
Total	1,977		

Source: *Annual Reports* of the Department of Labor of Puerto Rico.

Approximately twenty percent of the men who secured positions through this agency were laborers and construction workers; sixteen percent were laundry workers; eight percent were porters,

[5] *Ibid.*, 1935-36, p. 27. J. M. Vivaldi stated that unskilled WPA workers were receiving $55 for fifteen days of work each month and that a family of five was getting from $50 to $60 per month from the Home Relief Bureau. Families on relief also receive medical care and clothing allowances.

[6] Classification of occupations is not the same in these reports; those given in this table are approximate.

errand boys, and domestics; and six percent were hotel workers. Less than three percent of the total number employed were sent to offices or clerical positions. The small inclination of the Puerto Rican to do agricultural work is shown by the fact that in six years only eleven workers of this class were placed. Of the total number of women employed, approximately forty-two percent were domestics; twenty percent were needleworkers and hand sewers; and twenty percent were garment workers. About eighty percent of all the women workers from Puerto Rico found positions in these three occupations. It will be observed that the occupations in which most of the applicants found work are those in which the wages are often notoriously low. Reference has already been made to the statement of this employment service in 1935-36 that the salaries at which the majority of the Puerto Rican people could be employed at that time were below the levels of the WPA and the Home Relief Bureau.

Although the conclusion does not necessarily follow that these occupational data of the Puerto Rican Employment Service are representative of the Harlem group, they are the most authoritative and complete information which can be obtained. To the Puerto Rican this office is much more than just an employment agency. It may help him collect his wages, advise him about a pension, assist him with a problem of relief, or perform any of various other necessary services for him. It affords the Puerto Rican an opportunity to discuss his problems with his own people in his own language. Considering the size of the Puerto Rican group in New York, the fact that as many as 5,000 persons have applied for work through this agency in one year, and 16,500 have applied for work during the period of about six years, indicates that it serves a large group of Puerto Rican workers.

The amount of homework now being done by Puerto Rican workers is not large. During the earlier years of the migration, such as 1925 or 1926, this type of work constituted a rather important source of earnings for many of the Puerto Rican families. Conditions in this work, which was often hat making or home sewing of some sort, were similar to those in Puerto Rico in that the worker was paid very little and the contractor took a very large share of the total proceeds. Owing to the increasing restrictions put upon this kind of labor by the Department of Labor of New York State, the total number in the city doing homework has dwindled rapidly; but of the total the Puerto Rican proportion was greater in 1936 and 1937 than it was in a year such as 1933. The numbers of Puerto Ricans engaged in this kind of work during the years from 1933 to 1936 in New York City were as follows: in 1933, 402; in 1934, 318; in 1935, 228; in 1936, 327.[7] Most of the homework done at the present time by the Puerto Ricans is needlework. The making of lamp shades is another class of work which many Puerto Rican women have recently taken up. The homeworker is paid by the piece and the weekly earnings are extremely small. The Department of Labor of New York State, in its recent studies of various homework industries, such as those of men's clothing, men's neckwear, flowers, and feathers, found no Puerto Ricans engaged in these lines. The amount of homework now being done by the Puerto Rican group is small, even though the figures given above might not represent all persons engaged, because of "bootleg" homework; that is, work not done in accordance with the registration requirement of the labor laws of New York State.

HANDICAPS IN OBTAINING WORK

One of the greatest handicaps of the Puerto Rican worker in New York, which is evident from the facts already given, is his lack of skill. This difficulty is stressed in almost all of the reports which have been made by the Puerto Rican Employment Service. Even in such periods of unemployment as the year 1932, the service reported that it was unable to fill many positions because of the lack of workers who were fully qualified.[8] In the annual report for the year 1935-36, it is stated that an industrial school in Puerto Rico, the need for which had been stressed in former reports, is an absolute necessity, and that newcomers from Puerto Rico "at present and for a long time to come, will not be able to earn their living at decent wages if they are not well equipped

[7] Information furnished by the Department of Labor of New York State, June, 1937.
[8] Commissioner of Labor of Puerto Rico, *Annual Report*, 1931-32, p. 38.

Occupations and Employment

to compete in this labor market."[9] The need for industrial training in practically all lines of work would have to be met some time before the migrant leaves the island. In addition to the importance of a knowledge of English, it would be necessary to emphasize conditions and trade practices found in New York. Those familiar with conditions found among the Puerto Rican migrants are convinced that practical training in mechanical trades, automobile and garage work, garment making, domestic service, and other similar occupations would go a long way toward meeting the difficulties encountered by the newly arrived worker from the island.

Much of the skill which the worker may have had on the island is useless under the different conditions in New York. He may find conditions so completely changed, and the manner of doing the work so different that it is almost necessary for him to re-learn whatever trade he might have had. This situation is illustrated in domestic work, in which a large number of Puerto Rican women are employed. In the first place, if the worker speaks only Spanish the market for this work is very limited. Moreover, whatever the merits of Puerto Rican and American methods of household management may be, they are at least very different. The average domestic worker from the island seeking employment in New York, unless she were employed by a Spanish-speaking family of the lower-income group, would require training. The average Puerto Rican woman knows very little about the cooking of American food. Some of the vegetables found in Puerto Rico are unknown in New York. The Puerto Rican cook uses too much grease or lard to suit the American taste. It is the general practice in Puerto Rico to wash all dishes in cold water and allow them to dry without the use of cloths. In cleaning the house, water is usually poured in liberal quantities upon the tile floors and taken up by the hands or feet with large cloths.

The handicap of language difficulty is a factor mentioned in many of the reports of the Puerto Rican Employment Service already referred to. As has been stated in a previous chapter, the census enumeration of 1930 showed that about eighty percent of

[9] *Ibid.*, p. 29.

the people on the island do not speak English. The actual number who speak English well is much smaller than is indicated by this figure. Not even all of the people of the professional classes, university students, and those engaged in trade in Puerto Rico have a ready command of English. The Puerto Rican worker must not only "speak" English, but he must speak it well enough to compete with other applicants. This inability to speak English well is one of the most important reasons why the Puerto Rican has to accept poorly paid and unskilled work.

Without doubt the poor economic conditions in Puerto Rico, probably assisted by the tropical climate, deprive many of the workers coming from the island of robust health. Poorly balanced diets, often the lack of food in sufficient quantities, together with infestations of intestinal parasites, are not conducive to high industrial efficiency. It will be shown in a following chapter that a large proportion of the group in New York still suffer from intestinal parasites.[10] The majority of the people on the island have been infested at one time or another. For example, tests made in past years have disclosed that practically all of the people in some communities had hookworm.[11] All of these facts would show that the average worker who has just arrived from the island is probably at a disadvantage as compared with workers of greater vitality and better health. It could hardly be expected that a worker who has suffered the economic distress which has been the lot of many of the people of Puerto Rico would generally be able to enter employment calling for the greatest strength and endurance. The high incidence of tuberculosis among them, when known to employers, also has an effect upon their desirability for certain kinds of work. Some of the American employers also say that the Puerto Rican worker is too small for heavy work.[12] Puerto Ricans resent such statements, and call attention to the difficult and heavy work performed by them on the island.

[10] See p. 121.
[11] U. S. Department of Labor, Children's Bureau, *Child Welfare in the Insular Possessions of the United States*, p. 38.
[12] For example, see the statement of Rudolph Reimer, District Commissioner of Immigration, New York *Times*, May 20, 1937, that the free entry of Puerto Ricans to the United States is one of the biggest problems confronting immigration officials, and that because of his poor physique and health, the migrant is unable to perform ordinary labor.

Occupations and Employment 79

Puerto Rican workers in New York are not generally organized;[13] comparatively few belong to a trade union. The unions which have the largest numbers of Puerto Ricans are one branch of the International Cigar Maker's Union and the Spanish-speaking branch of the International Ladies' Garment Workers' Union. There is discrimination against the Puerto Rican in many of the American unions.[14] A Puerto Rican labor official who has dealt with the labor problems of the Puerto Ricans in New York for many years explained that this discrimination is usually shown when a company becomes unionized, the new union excluding the Puerto Rican workers.

There is often discrimination against the Puerto Rican worker on the basis of color. As was stated in a previous chapter, the entire group is sometimes referred to by Americans as "colored." One instance of this troublesome problem for the Puerto Rican came about a few years ago when a large religious organization in New York is said to have classified all of the Puerto Rican applicants in its employment division as "colored." Another agency which supplies domestic help reported that it is not unusual, when a woman calls by telephone to inquire about obtaining a Puerto Rican worker and is asked whether she prefers a white or colored Puerto Rican, for the woman to reply that, since she has asked for a Puerto Rican, of course she wants a colored person. An educated girl of a rather prominent Spanish-speaking family deeply resented being asked by a downtown employment agency if she were colored. A social worker reported that she had encountered difficulty on account of the fact that a Puerto Rican boy who had gone to a Civilian Conservation Corps camp was placed in the colored division. After a violent protest on his part, he was transferred to the white division, but this group would not accept him on friendly terms. Another worker told of a Brooklyn factory which put up a sign, "No Negroes or Porto Ricans Wanted." Instances of difficulty on account of color are so frequent that numerous examples could be given.

Although the Puerto Rican is an American citizen, there is

[13] Commissioner of Labor of Puerto Rico, *Annual Report*, 1934-35, p. 33.
[14] The Puerto Rican Employment Service states that this is not a general rule, but that many instances of discrimination can be found.

sometimes a prejudice against him on the basis that he is a "Spanish worker," or a "foreigner."[15] This feeling is also expressed in the strong preference for the "American type" worker. One Puerto Rican social worker who has lived in Harlem for many years commented upon this discrimination as follows: "One example of it is shown by the fact that Wall Street firms and brokerage houses will not employ an educated Puerto Rican even for a position where he could use his knowledge of Spanish to advantage. There is a distinct prejudice against him. This is shown also by calling for a 'Spanish-English Secretary, American Type Only.'" Except possibly for governmental work, the Puerto Rican's citizenship gives him little advantage in competition with workers from the other Latin-American countries. In fact, it appears that many employers class all Latin Americans together as one group of workers.

OTHER FACTORS RELATED TO EMPLOYMENT

Reports from employers concerning the Puerto Rican worker are conflicting. It must be recognized that many Puerto Ricans in New York have made a satisfactory adjustment and have held their positions for years. As might be expected, employers who have hired large groups of Puerto Ricans are reluctant to express an opinion. Some state that they are "entirely satisfactory"; others say, "We do not employ them any more." As with any unskilled group, there are reports that the Puerto Rican worker is inclined to lack ambition, to be undependable and unsteady. The real opinion of many employers may be deduced from the situation during the depression. The Puerto Ricans, for the most part, came to this country when there was an urgent demand for labor. In the depression several establishments hiring large numbers dismissed most of them. One factory denied that this was caused in any way by the work of the Puerto Ricans, but was because they thought it unwise to have too many workers of any one particular group. Another large chain restaurant stated that the Puerto Ricans were breaking too many dishes. Some of the people whom

[15] Commissioner of Labor, *Annual Report*, 1931-32, p. 38, and 1935-36, p. 27. For a general discussion of the problem of racial adjustment in industry, see Herman Feldman, *Racial Factors in American Industry*. Comment on the attitude toward the Spanish worker is given on p. 154.

they had discharged had been working for this concern for many years. A reason given by another employment manager was that the Puerto Ricans do not speak English well. A better explanation of the dismissal of Puerto Ricans in the depression is the fact that in many cases Puerto Ricans could be replaced by workers who had greater skill and experience than the Puerto Rican and who in the depression would work for as little money. One instance was found in which, due to misconduct on the part of several Puerto Ricans, the entire group working in an establishment was brought into disfavor. The opinion also exists that the Puerto Rican worker is inclined to be quick-tempered and sensitive. It is probably true that he is inclined to protest quickly against what he considers to be mistreatment. Often the reprimand of a foreman is construed by him to be an insult. This "sensitive disposition" sometimes involves him in difficulties with the management or with his fellow workers.

Discrimination and the failure on the part of the Puerto Rican migrant to realize his expectations in New York often cause feelings of resentment or bitterness. In the spring of 1937, a New York newspaper published some interesting interviews with a group of Puerto Ricans who were returning to the island. The following is typical of the reaction of the group: "We are very disappointed with New York. We thought this was the money center of the world. I worked in a bakery. My wife worked in a laundry. We did not like the climate."[16] Practically every member of the group commented upon the cold climate. Another person said: "I never want to see a fur coat again. I just want little clothes and warm sun." In another series of interviews, the following statement, secured from a young Puerto Rican woman in East Harlem, shows evidence of hardship and disappointment:[17]

I was brought to the United States by the American Cotton Growers Association with several thousand others to work on the farm in Arizona. We were promised three dollars a day. None of us were paid this sum. We were given provisions but no money. Some of the men managed to get back to Galveston, Texas, and worked their way home on a freight

[16] *World-Telegram*, March 24, 1937.
[17] William E. Hill, "Porto Rican Colonies in New York" (typewritten manuscript, 14 pp., on file in office of National Urban League).

line. Hundreds of them are still there in a very bad condition. . . . My brother sent me money to come to New York. Since coming to New York, I have been working as an operator in a shirt factory at ten dollars a week. We work nine hours a day with a half hour for lunch. I am not well, my sister is here and she is very ill. . . . My father is sixty-five years old and he cannot work.

All of the other interviews secured showed the serious problem of adjustment of the Puerto Rican to conditions in New York.

According to labor officials and Puerto Rican social workers in daily contact with the New York group, the Puerto Rican worker is not a strikebreaker. Almost without exception, his sympathies will be found on the side of the workers who are involved in an industrial dispute. This attitude exists despite his belief that the American union is unfriendly to him, and in spite of the fact that comparatively few Puerto Ricans belong to unions.[18] There may be some relation between this attitude and the existence of a strong socialist political party on the island.

The Puerto Rican worker who lives in Harlem and does unskilled work is bound to encounter group conflicts of one sort or another. The American Negro is inclined to resent all of the people from the West Indies because of their competition in the labor market. In the past years there has been a definite conflict between the colored worker from the West Indies and the colored group here.[19] The American Negro especially resents the worker from the British West Indies. His feeling may be shown by some of the terms he applies against him, such as "superior," "high-hat," "a pessimist," and "stiff British attitude." Because the Puerto Rican speaks Spanish, he is apt to encounter some of the same resentment. The Puerto Rican, if white or slightly colored, deeply resents any classification which places him with the Negro. There is a unanimity of opinion that the Puerto Rican gets along well with the Italian. Among the Spanish-speaking groups, there is considerable provincial feeling and criticism. In Puerto Rico, there is often criticism of their nearest neighbors, the people of

[18] Information obtained by interviews and later checked with officials of the Puerto Rican Employment Service.
[19] For a fuller discussion of this attitude see W. A. Domingo, "The Tropics in New York," *Survey*, Vol. III, No. 11 (March 1, 1925), p. 650.

Santo Domingo. In New York, Cubans and Puerto Ricans often find fault with each other. Boat crews made up of Cubans and Puerto Ricans often have difficulties. The only racial groups, however, which the Puerto Ricans really seem to regard with disfavor are the Orientals. If thrown into close contact with a large group of Filipinos, for example, they might easily develop an attitude similar to that which the Mexicans in some sections have already developed. The Mexicans are reported to "have a grudge against the Filipinos."[20]

THE MIGRANT'S POOR ECONOMIC STATUS AS SHOWN BY DEPENDENCY

On account of the conditions found in Puerto Rico, poverty would be expected in any group of people coming from there to New York. In New York there is not only poverty among the Puerto Rican families, but many of them are dependent upon the various welfare agencies. An adequate discussion of this problem is beyond the scope of this study, and might well be the subject of a separate investigation. It is intended here to bring out how these migrants, on account of their dependency, present a problem for New York, and to discuss the relation of this dependency to the general economic status of the workers. The problem of relief has been associated with the migration of the Puerto Ricans for many years, and has confronted all of the welfare agencies in New York. The suggestion that the Puerto Ricans are "draining" relief funds and that many of them have come to New York without resources, expecting to be taken care of in some way, in order to escape from worse circumstances on the island is frequently encountered.[21]

Since the Department of Public Welfare of New York City does not publish statistics of the number of families on home relief according to racial groups, the actual number of Puerto Rican families receiving aid at the present time or in past years is un-

[20] Feldman, *op. cit.*, pp. 100-101. In 1931, one person was killed and three were wounded in what was described by the press as a Filipino-Spanish American race riot.—New York *Times,* July 16, 1931.

[21] New York *World-Telegram,* May 24, 1935. This article suggests that many Puerto Ricans are being assisted to move to New York in order to obtain public relief and describes the poor conditions under which they live.

known. During the worst periods of the depression, so large a proportion of the population of the Puerto Rican settlement in Harlem was receiving relief that the Department of Health believes that a group drawn from relief lists for the purpose of making tests for tuberculosis was fairly representative of the area.[22] The Puerto Rican case load of the private agency in these years was also abnormally high. Although the number of persons born in Puerto Rico constituted only about six-tenths of one percent of the total population of New York City in 1930, the records of one large and well-known private charity agency show that in 1933 Puerto Rican families constituted six and one-half percent of its entire case load.

Even though there has been a remarkable improvement in business conditions as compared with the worst years of the depression, the number of Puerto Rican families receiving relief is still abnormally high. This fact is clearly brought out by figures secured from the Emergency Relief Bureau of New York City in July of 1937. At that time, it was estimated by the heads of four district relief offices in Harlem that there were 6,350 Puerto Rican families on relief.[23] In 1930 the number of people in Manhattan who were born in Puerto Rico constituted only one and eight-tenths percent of the total population of the borough. The number of Puerto Rican families in the Harlem area alone which were on relief in July, 1937, constituted almost eleven per cent of the total number of families receiving relief in the whole borough of Manhattan. A similar, or possibly even higher, proportion of the Puerto Rican families in Brooklyn are receiving relief. If five is taken to be the number of individuals in the family of average size (the figure indicated by the census of 1930), there were approximately 32,000 persons in Puerto Rican families in the Harlem district on relief in July of 1937.[24]

This problem of the needy Puerto Rican family in New York is not one which has arisen entirely with the depression. It existed in a rather serious form in such years as 1928 and 1929. With discrimination and lack of employment opportunities, it might be

[22] See Milbank Memorial Fund, *Quarterly Bulletin,* July, 1933, p. 234.

[23] These estimates were compiled from case records and other data.

[24] The average size of families according to the 1930 census was almost exactly five for the area of settlement described in the chapter on Housing; see p. 93.

Occupations and Employment 85

considered unfair to point to statistics of dependency in 1932 and 1933 and attempt to judge the success or failure of a group living in Harlem by these figures. All of the Harlem section suffered the severest hardships, and unemployment in the area was general. It will be found, however, that prior to the depression the problem of the Puerto Rican family was becoming one of serious concern for the charity organizations. For the fiscal year 1927-28, for example, about five percent of the entire case load of one of the largest private charity organizations in New York was made up of Puerto Ricans. For the same year the percentage of the total cases of this organization in the Harlem district was over twenty percent. During these years, there was also a high percentage of Puerto Rican cases in the Navy Yard section of the Brooklyn district.[25] Other private charity organizations showed a similar proportion of their case loads to be Puerto Ricans. Figures for years prior to this time also disclose that the Puerto Rican case load was abnormally high. In 1930, at a meeting of social workers of a large organization, Rose McHugh stated that the needy Puerto Rican family presented the biggest social-work problem in New York City at that time, and that it appeared that among the Puerto Ricans dependency synchronized with long periods of residence in this country.[26]

Although it began earlier, the problem of the needy Puerto Rican in New York culminated in 1930, and from this time it has received the attention of special committees of the Welfare Council of New York. After several conferences in the early part of 1930, the Puerto Rican Community Committee was formed.[27] This committee began immediately to assemble data and to make plans to handle the problem. As time went on, the necessity for the work of this committee decreased because the program of relief was

[25] From the report of the Puerto Rican Community Committee, April, 1930 (unpublished).
[26] Rose J. McHugh, "Social Welfare among the Spanish-speaking People," Sixteenth Session, *National Conference of Catholic Charities*, 1930, p. 277. Miss McHugh is listed in the directory of social work as Assistant Commissioner of the Division of Administration of State Institutions under the State Board of Social Welfare.
[27] Welfare Council, Puerto Rican Community Committee, *Annual Report*, 1933-34. The Welfare Council is a coördinating organization of private social agencies and should not be confused with departments of the city government.

greatly expanded and because migration from the island became negligible. The plan of this committee to publish a handbook for the use of the newly arrived Puerto Rican has not yet been carried out. The committee has, however, been responsible in part for the special tuberculosis case-finding studies undertaken in later years by the Department of Health.

The relief problem in 1930 arose because of the large number of families which were coming at that time, and also because of the very insecure economic basis of those who were already here. In the years 1929 and 1930, there was a large movement of people from the island.[28] Migration in 1930 was even greater than in 1929. Instances of Puerto Rican families seeking aid from some charity organization after being here for only a week or two were not infrequent. Many of these families were desperate. On account of the poor economic status of the average Puerto Rican in New York, he was among the first to fall victim of the depression.

The Puerto Rican in New York presents difficulties not only because his economic situation is usually desperate, but because of the character of the family group. As has been said, the newcomers usually come, one by one, through the help of relatives. Social workers report that suddenly from time to time an additional member of the family may appear. It is, for this reason, next to impossible to plan for the family a budget, which will last for any period of time. The Puerto Ricans also have a practice of sharing whatever they have with their unfortunate relatives and friends. If a child needs a home, these poor people will provide for it in some way.

The degree of poverty existing on the island has had a close bearing upon the relief problem existing among the Puerto Ricans here. The general relief which has been given in Puerto Rico has practically stopped at the present time. The appropriations for public works have now been almost exhausted. Social workers and others are now asking, "What is next in Puerto Rico?"[29] Because of the poverty on the island and because the passage amounts to

[28] Table 14, p. 54.
[29] See D. Bourne, "Puerto Rico's Predicament," *Survey*, July, 1936. Mrs. Bourne stated at that time that the minimum amount for subsistence for a family of five was about $30 per month. The amount of relief per family given in Puerto Rico at that time was from seventy-five cents to one dollar per week.

only forty dollars, New York may soon experience another acute situation as a result of a new inrush of Puerto Ricans. The requirements for eligibility for relief in New York have recently been changed from the former two-year period of continuous residence without public relief to a one-year period.[30] Due to the facts that Puerto Rico is financially unable to provide for its great mass of poverty-stricken people and the number of people on the island is increasing at such a rapid rate, the problem of relief for the needy family which has moved from the island to New York will not only continue, but may become of greater consequence than it is at the present time.

SUMMARY AND CONCLUSION

From the standpoint of employment and economic security, the migration of the Puerto Rican worker to New York is, at best, only a partial solution to his problem. He is a newcomer in the labor market, has little skill or industrial training, suffers a language handicap, and is often still affected by the poor health conditions found on the island. Having moved to New York to earn the high money wages of which he has been told, he now finds that what he terms "prejudice" and "discrimination" prevent the fulfillment of his expectations. The Puerto Rican who is not entirely white finds a new discrimination based on color. Facing these difficulties, the worker, if he is employed at all, usually has to do unskilled labor at wages which are notoriously low.

With few resources and unequipped to enter the new labor market, the Puerto Rican worker often becomes dependent. Prior to the depression, dependency was associated with the movement of people from the island to New York, and at the present time the proportion of Puerto Rican families, according to population receiving relief, is abnormally high. It is probable that the majority of the Puerto Rican families in some sections of the city are now dependent. This situation suggests the additional problem which could result from an increased migration from the island in the near future.

There are no statistical data which show the extent, if any, to

[30] Families not having residence requirements may be temporarily taken care of by the state of New York.

which the group as a whole has improved its economic status by moving to New York. The success of the worker is largely an individual matter, and depends to some extent upon the year in which he came. As a whole, the group appears to be gaining very little economic security here. In spite of this fact, there may have been some improvement in the economic status of the worker in New York over the wretched conditions which he left on the island. The fact of the continued migration, itself, would lead to this conclusion.

Although there are many individual cases which show an improved economic status as a result of migration—especially among the workers who came in the decade 1920-30 and were able to establish themselves in prosperous times, and always among the skilled workers who speak English—the unskilled workers by no means solve their economic difficulties by moving to New York City.

CHAPTER VI

The Housing of the Puerto Rican Worker in New York City

AS THE amount of money which a worker is able to earn largely determines the character of his home and the section of the city in which he lives, a discussion of housing logically follows that of occupations and economic status. The housing of the rather large group of migrants from Puerto Rico is extremely important both to the worker and his family and also to the city. Students of housing problems have, over a long period of years, accumulated convincing evidence of the relation of the housing in certain sections of a city to the health and moral life of the people of that section. Health is affected by a lack of sunlight and fresh air, dampness, overcrowding, and the unsanitary conditions found in slum areas.[1] The moral life of the family is affected by associations in slum neighborhoods and by overcrowding in the family quarters. The devastating effect of the slum upon children may almost offset the work of educational programs. People living in houses without sunlight, infested with vermin, and without even necessary sanitary conveniences may not only fail to carry out their duties of citizenship, but may find in these conditions reasons for revolt and for the development of radical organizations.

The city as a whole is also affected by the slum conditions of these areas. Disease germs have little regard for the imaginary lines of the ward or health district. Criminals do not always choose their own neighborhoods for their crimes. The large industrial city of the North, like the Southern city with its colored sections, is beginning to realize that it cannot escape the consequences of

---

[1] "A slum is most simply defined as housing (on whatever scale) so inadequate or so deteriorated as to endanger the health, safety, or morals of its inhabitants." Edith Elmer Wood, "Slums and Blighted Areas in the United States," *Bulletin No. 1,* Federal Emergency Administration of Public Works, Housing Division, 1935, p. 3.

the poor housing, unsanitary conditions, and complex neighborhood situations surrounding people in certain areas.

Although tenement-housing studies are by no means a new thing in New York (some of the surveys date back as far as 1853), there has been, during the last three or four years, what is probably a more active interest in housing than at any other period of our history. This interest in housing has been stimulated by the prolonged depression with its program of public works, the search for survey work which would employ people in a time of emergency, the interest of the Federal government in housing, and the realization by many persons that private capital and initiative alone cannot be relied upon to remove the slum areas from a city such as New York. It was brought out by the census of 1930 that about twenty percent of the tenement families were paying less than thirty dollars per month rent, which was considered to indicate an unsatisfactory standard at that time; and that thirty-four percent paid between thirty and forty dollars rent, which, in many cases, indicated poor housing and low standards. In 1933, the Land Utilization Committee of New York carried out certain research projects dealing with density of population, gain and loss of population between districts, median rentals, vacancies, a special study of the Bronx, and a survey of the previous studies which had been made by organizations and civic groups.[2] The work of the Slum Clearance Committee followed in the latter part of 1933, and made use of and extended the work of the former committee. A large range of information was developed for selected areas, including studies of the Negro and foreign-born populations, accidents and fires, infant mortality, tuberculosis, venereal disease, and crime. The next important work was done at about the time the New York City Housing Authority came into existence in February of 1934. In turn, this organization inherited the valuable work completed by the former committees. Probably never before has work of such magnitude on housing been undertaken. Their publications in 1934 included *Real Property Inventory of New York* and *Har-*

[2] An excellent summary of surveys on housing in New York and other cities is given by Dr. Edith Elmer Wood, *op. cit.* The information given above has been taken from this source.

lem, 1934.[3] Another important study dealing with adult and juvenile delinquency was that made by Halpern and others under the title of *The Slum and Crime.*[4] An exhaustive study of the entire housing and slum problem with special reference to New York City, not connected with the New York Housing Authority, but representing the combined work of many scholars, was published in 1936 by James Ford, under the title of *Slums and Housing.*[5] These surveys and publications afford recent statistical material in greater detail than has ever before been available and make possible, by the segregation of data, the study and comparison of particular areas of the city.

AREA IN HARLEM WITH LARGE PUERTO RICAN POPULATION

A general statement about the place of settlement of the Puerto Rican people in New York City, as disclosed by the census enumeration of 1930, was given in Chapter IV. The data given showed that there was a marked tendency for the Puerto Rican to concentrate in certain areas, and that the largest and most important settlement was in the lower and eastern sections of Harlem. A second district which had numerous Puerto Ricans was in Brooklyn along the water front from the Navy Yard south to Gowanus Canal. This tendency of the group to concentrate in certain districts was shown by the fact that about seventy percent of the total number of Puerto Ricans living in New York City in 1930 had settled in four statistical areas, as shown by the census.[6] In order to study the housing of the districts where the Puerto Ricans live, it is now necessary to discuss these areas in more detail.

The first settlement of Puerto Ricans in large numbers in this city was in a section of old-style tenement houses in the neighborhood of 101st and 102d Streets at about Third Avenue.[7] Since

[3] Published for the New York City Housing Authority by the Polygraphic Company of America, New York, 1934. *Harlem, 1934,* was a similar publication dealing with the Harlem area.

[4] I. W. Halpern, John N. Stanislaus, and Bernard Botein. Published for the New York Housing Authority.

[5] Harvard University Press, Cambridge, Mass. (2 vols.)

[6] The boundaries of these areas were given on p. 63.

[7] The earliest migrants from Puerto Rico appear to have been a group of cigar makers who settled in the Lower East Side. There is still a fairly large Spanish-speaking settlement in the neighborhood around Cherry Street.

the beginning of the settlement, not much expansion has taken place to the south. As large numbers continued to come from the island, the settlement was extended north to the area around the northern boundaries of Central Park. Here the Puerto Ricans found, as a rule, much better apartments, but also higher rents. They also found conflicts with Jewish people who were at the time living in some of the better buildings. In the early twenties, old residents of the area say that the conflict between members of the two groups almost approached race riots. After once gaining entrance to this section of Harlem, the Puerto Rican has been free to move about over a large area. Puerto Ricans, together with other Spanish-speaking groups, have now extended the settlement northward to meet a highly congested area which is almost entirely colored, at about 125th Street, and an Italian and foreign-born white settlement on the east. On the west, the extension of the area has been blocked by the natural boundaries of Morningside Park. Facing congested populations on the north and east, Puerto Rican families are now gradually moving into areas north of Morningside Park and into Washington Heights. At the present time in Washington Heights, the Puerto Rican often has difficulty in securing an apartment. The question of color is sometimes the deciding factor against him, and the tenants in other ways are much more highly selected than in the Harlem section.

There is a general feeling among the Puerto Ricans in New York that discrimination exists against them in the matter of housing. Even in Puerto Rico, the visitor is often asked by people of the low-income group who are of mixed blood if it is true that Americans force certain racial groups to live in particular areas of a city. A good example of the resentment which has been caused by this discrimination was shown by a cartoon which appeared in the Spanish newspaper, *La Prensa,* a few years ago. One half of the cartoon pictured a prosperous fat American in a Spanish-speaking country, with a huge cigar in his mouth and American dollars falling out of his pockets, saying in incorrect Spanish that he had come to get "muchos pesos" and that he wanted a fine place to live. Two little Spaniards were bowing and bidding him welcome, "Aqui tiene Vd. su casa." The other half of the picture, which was

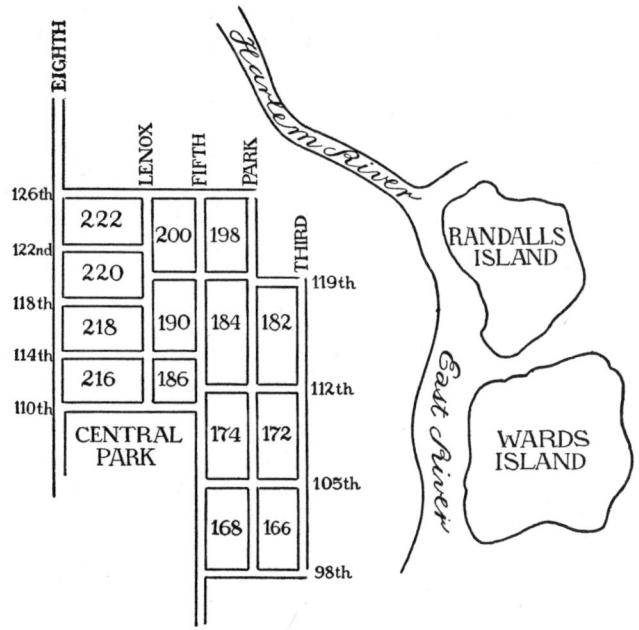

FIGURE 1. AREA OF PUERTO RICAN SETTLEMENT IN HARLEM, BY CENSUS TRACTS

BOUNDARIES

Beginning at Eighth Avenue on East 126th Street, West 126th Street and East 126th Street to Park Avenue, Park Avenue to East 119th Street, East 119th Street to Third Avenue, Third Avenue to East 98th Street, 98th to Fifth Avenue, Fifth Avenue to 110th Street, 110th Street to Eighth Avenue, and along Eighth Avenue to 126th Street.

CENSUS TRACTS

| 166 | 172 | 182 | 186 | 198 | 216 | 220 |
| 168 | 174 | 184 | 190 | 200 | 218 | 222 |

marked "Washington Heights," showed an American woman waving a broom and saying with anger to some prospective tenants, "!Fuera [away, get out]! No Spanish people are allowed here." In spite of the difficulty found by the Puerto Rican worker in some sections, however, the group is spreading out to various parts of the city, but their principal place of settlement is still confined to Harlem and the Navy Yard section of Brooklyn.

In order to study the housing of this group, a rather large area has been selected in which there are numerous Puerto Ricans and other Spanish-speaking people. The basis for this selection has, for the most part, been based on information furnished by the Department of Health. A recent map study of the area by type of population, together with information obtained from social workers and institutions in the district, has been used to define the area in a more exact manner. A discussion of the method and material used for the selection of the Harlem area to be studied will be found in Appendix A. Since the statistical units of the census and the Department of Health, such as the "statistical areas" and the "health areas," are too large, it has been necessary to set out the place of settlement in terms of the census tract.[8] The boundaries and the census tracts selected for the Lower Harlem area are indicated in Figure 1.

No great degree of exactness has been possible in the selection of the area to be studied, as many Puerto Ricans will be found living outside the boundaries given, and, of course, many other racial groups will be found within it. Furthermore, it is difficult to say just where particular groups reside on account of the shifting of the population which is constantly going on within an area such as Harlem. This area, although containing numerous other groups, is the one which has the largest Puerto Rican settlement in Manhattan and a large proportion of all of the Puerto Rican people living in the entire city.

It will be found from an examination of the area selected that certain census tracts contain larger proportions of Puerto Rican and other Spanish-speaking people than do others. This fact cannot be shown by the census data because Puerto Ricans are native-

[8] Also called "sanitary districts" in various publications of New York City.

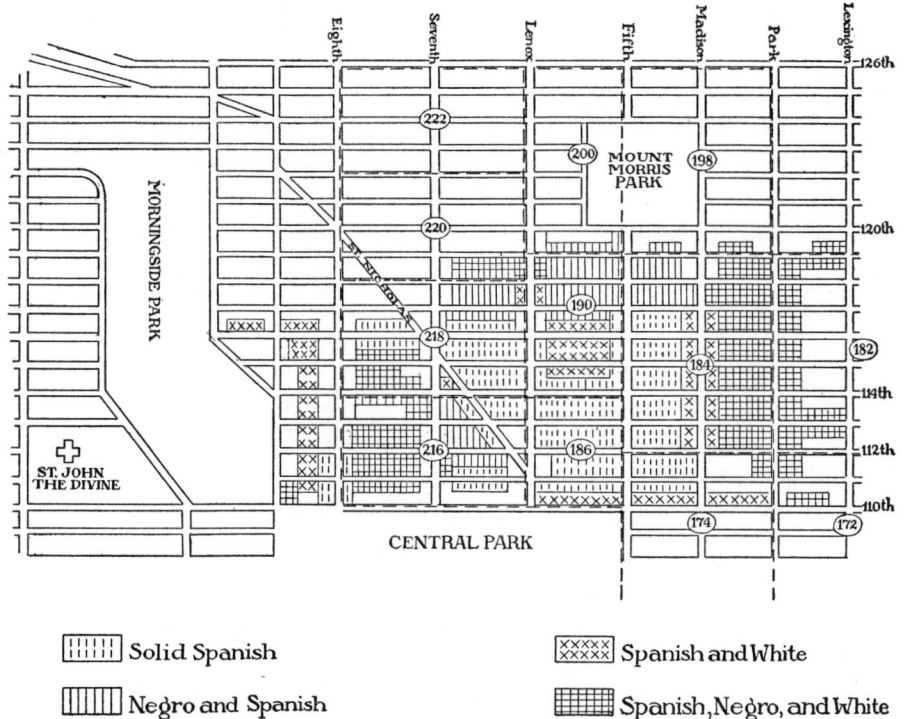

FIGURE 2. SETTLEMENT OF SPANISH-SPEAKING RACIAL GROUPS IN THE LOWER HARLEM AREA, NEW YORK CITY

Source: Adapted from a map study prepared by the New York Urban League which appeared in the *Sun,* March 22, 1935, in the New York *Times,* March 24, 1935, and in Ford, *Slums and Housing,* I, 323.

Classifications of racial groups other than Spanish-speaking are omitted. Census tracts are indicated by broken lines. In the map, language takes precedence over color.

born, and no separate classification is made for them. One area of concentration of Puerto Ricans and other Spanish-speaking people is centered around 115th and 116th Streets and Fifth Avenue. According to social workers, to Puerto Ricans living in the area, and to actual appearances, this part of the settlement, sometimes known as the "116th Street Center," probably contains the highest percentage of Spanish-speaking people in the entire Harlem area. The tendency for Spanish-speaking people to concentrate in this area is also brought out by a recent map study by blocks according to the character of the population, shown by Figure 2. When the census tracts are drawn on this study, it is clear that census tracts 184, 186, 190, 216, and 218 all have very large numbers of Spanish-speaking people. Tracts 184, 186, and 190 are in the center of this concentration at 116th Street. There is also another part of the area selected which is almost entirely Puerto Rican. The center of this second concentration is around 101st and 102d Streets and about Third Avenue. Census tracts 166 and 172 have very large numbers of Puerto Ricans.

In Harlem, the settlement of the Puerto Rican with some degree of Negro blood and the Puerto Rican Negro, as a rule, tends to follow the general area of the settlement of white Puerto Ricans and other Spanish-speaking people. The colored Puerto Rican does not separate himself from other Puerto Ricans and go to live in the congested sections of northern Harlem, but settles with them. In fact, comparatively few colored Puerto Ricans will be found in the areas where there are the most congested settlements of American Negroes. Color in all of the selected area in Harlem is often only a matter of degree. Language among the group in Harlem is more important in determining the area of settlement than the degree of color. The colored Puerto Rican will, therefore, be found settling with white Puerto Ricans and other Spanish-speaking people, and all of them tend to concentrate in the same general area.

The population of this area is badly crowded. Out of the fourteen census tracts selected for study, eleven had the highest residential population density classification of the *Real Property Inventory,* that is, from 200 to 500 persons per acre. Two of the census tracts showed a population density of from 100 to 200 per-

Housing in New York

sons per acre, and only one census tract in the entire area had less than 100 persons per acre.[9]

GENERAL CHARACTERISTICS OF HOUSING IN THE SELECTED AREA OF HARLEM

Like almost any other area of this size in the city of New York, this area contains a great variety of housing conditions. One of the areas in which housing is particularly poor is the Puerto Rican settlement around 100th and 101st Streets, east of Madison Avenue. A large proportion of the houses in this vicinity are old, unsanitary, and not in good repair. Many of the apartments have only one outside window. North of this section, in the center of the greatest concentration, around 116th Street, the buildings appear to be somewhat better, but many of them are the old railroad type of apartment with two windows in the front and air shafts. This type of structure is predominant in the entire area selected. Along 110th Street, north of Central Park, the buildings are far better than in other sections. Most of the buildings in a neighborhood such as that of 114th Street and St. Nicholas Avenue are large, expensive, and modern apartments.

The general housing conditions of a selected area are best judged by a comparison with those of other areas. There is danger in finding fault with the age and condition of the buildings and the extent of crowding in an area without showing whether or not these conditions are worse than those found in other areas or in the city as a whole. In New York, examples of poor housing may be found in almost any part of the city.

The data used for this comparison have been taken from the *New York Real Property Inventory of 1934*. A table showing the information taken from this source will be found in Appendix B. In this table, information is first given for the selected area in Harlem. This is followed by similar data for the Brooklyn area,[10] the entire borough of Manhattan, and the Lower East Side and the Central Harlem health districts.[11] Since the housing in a large

[9] *Real Property Inventory*, Borough of Manhattan, map, p. XLIII.
[10] The Brooklyn area is defined in a later section of this chapter. See p. 104.
[11] The health district is an area used by the Department of Health in its program of neighborhood health development. It is selected by the Department on account

part of Brooklyn differs so materially from that of these other areas, no comparison is made with this borough. The comparison of the selected areas with those of the Lower East Side and the Central Harlem health districts is a comparison with substandard areas rather than with areas where housing conditions are desirable. Both of these districts have well-recognized housing problems. These districts have problems similar to the areas selected on account of the fact that the income of the average family is generally low, and that they are congested. It should also be noted that the Central Harlem health district includes a part of the area selected in Harlem.[12]

There has been a selection of such data from the *Real Property Inventory* as would bring out the character of housing facilities. First, the character of the housing may be judged by the age of the buildings, and next, by their condition; that is, whether they are in good condition, need only minor repairs, need major repairs, or are unfit for use. The character of the housing of the neighborhood may also be judged by the number of vacancies. Sanitary conveniences and modern improvements are another criterion. The amount of rental paid will show the price of the kind of facilities offered in these sections, and at the same time afford another basis for judging the housing. Extremely low rentals usually, but not always, indicate unsatisfactory housing. Since there is a difference between the definition of a family in the 1930 census and that in the 1934 *Real Property Inventory,* which will be explained, an increase in the number of families shown by enumeration in 1934 over that of 1930 gives some indication of the practice of families living together.

Using the above criteria, the character of housing in the selected area in Harlem may be summarized as follows (see table, Appendix B):

---

of population, particular health problems, and other factors, and affords an important basis for the classification of statistical data. Manhattan is divided into seven health districts. The boundaries of the Lower East Side and the Central Harlem health districts and the census tracts included in them will be found in Appendix C.

[12] From 110th Street to 126th Street between Fifth and Eighth Avenues and also from 119th Street and 126th Street between Fifth and Park Avenues. The remaining part of the selected area is included in what is known as the East Harlem district.

Housing in New York

1. Age of Buildings

Only about one and one-half percent of the buildings have been built within the last ten years. Ninety percent of all the buildings in the area are thirty-five or more years old. The proportion of old structures is greater than in Manhattan in general and is slightly higher than in the areas of the Lower East Side or Central Harlem. The area selected is definitely one of old structures.

2. Condition of Buildings

About thirteen percent of the buildings are in good condition, seventy percent need minor repairs, fifteen percent need major repairs, and less than three percent are unfit for use. In the borough of Manhattan, about one-fourth of all the buildings were classified as being in good condition. The proportion needing minor repairs is much greater than in Manhattan in general and is greater than in the other areas. The proportion of buildings classified as unfit for use is much lower than in Manhattan in general, and is about the same as in the Central Harlem district. The Lower East Side showed a much higher proportion of buildings in this classification than the area selected in Harlem. On the whole, the condition of the buildings is that of a substandard area.

3. Vacancies

In 1934 about fifteen percent of the total number of family quarters were vacant. No large difference existed in the proportion of vacancies in the selected area in Harlem and in the borough of Manhattan. The proportion of vacancies was the same as that of Central Harlem and was considerably less than that of the Lower East Side.

4. Equipment (mechanical refrigeration, baths, and toilets)

About ten percent of the occupied family quarters had mechanical refrigeration as compared with thirty percent for Manhattan. In other words, only about one-third as many of the occupied family quarters had mechanical refrigeration as in the entire area of Manhattan. The area was, however, slightly better off in this respect than Central Harlem and the Lower East Side. The proportion of family quarters which had either a tub or a shower was much higher in the area selected than in the borough as a whole. Only about one-half of the family quarters had this convenience in the Lower East Side district. Both the area selected and Central Harlem made a good showing in this respect. The same conclusions apply to the proportion of family quarters which had no private indoor toilet.

5. *Increase in Number of Families*

There was an increase of about seven percent in the number of families between the time of the census of 1930 and that of the New York *Real Property Inventory* in the entire borough of Manhattan. In the area selected in Harlem, however, there was an increase of approximately fourteen and one-half percent. The Lower East Side showed an increase of six percent, and the Central Harlem district of twelve percent. As will be explained later, this apparent increase in population is not real, but results from the difference in the definition of the family used in the two enumerations and may result largely from the practice of families living together, or "doubling up," as it is sometimes called.

6. *Rentals*

About fifteen percent of the rentals were under twenty dollars a month, thirty-nine percent were twenty to under thirty dollars per month, thirty-five percent were thirty dollars to under fifty dollars per month, and the balance over fifty dollars. Fifty-four percent of the entire number of rentals for family quarters were under thirty dollars per month.

PERCENTAGE OF FAMILIES PAYING RENT UNDER $30 A MONTH

Area	Percent
Selected area in Harlem	54.74
Selected area in Brooklyn	71.83
Manhattan	45.84
Lower East Side	79.63
Central Harlem	34.18

The figures given above do indicate poor standards for the Brooklyn area and Lower East Side. In Central Harlem, the small number of rentals under thirty dollars per month does not necessarily signify good housing conditions. The same factors which

Housing in New York

cause rentals to be high for the facilities given and their condition in Central Harlem would influence conditions in the selected area. The area selected is a comparatively high rental area with the average rental tending to be less than that found in Central Harlem.

The proportion of rentals of less than three dollars per room, which usually indicates quarters unfit for occupancy, is only four percent. Although this is greater than the proportion in Manhattan in general, it is less than that shown in the Brooklyn area and the Lower East Side. Twenty-seven percent of the total rentals per room are five and under six dollars per room, and nineteen percent of these rentals are from six to seven dollars per room. The rental per room is higher than that of the Lower East Side, but is lower than that of Central Harlem.

EVIDENCE OF CROWDING AS SHOWN BY SIZE OF FAMILIES AND THE PRACTICE OF FAMILIES LIVING TOGETHER

Data taken from the census of 1930 show that the Puerto Rican settlement is made up of large families. The following figures of the number of families in various groups bring out a comparison of the selected area with all of Manhattan:

Size of Family	Selected Area in Harlem	Percent	Manhattan	Percent
1 to 4 persons	21,666	67.6	370,298	79.0
5 to 8 persons	9,431	29.4	91,715	19.5
9 persons and over	944	3.0	6,943	1.5
Total	32,041	100.0	468,956	100.0

The very large family, with nine or more persons, is about twice as prevalent in the area selected as in all of Manhattan.

There are also families of very large size in those areas where there appears to be the greatest concentration of Puerto Ricans and other Spanish-speaking people (tracts 166, 172, 184, 186, 190). See Table 19 (p. 103). In none of these tracts did the classification of nine persons and over include less than three percent of the total number of families. The classification of families containing from five to eight persons in these census tracts include, with one exception, one-third or more of the total number of families.

There are also some statistical data which indicate that the area is one in which there are many families living temporarily together or doubling up. This is brought out on account of a difference in the definition of a family in the *Real Property Inventory* of 1934 and that in the census of 1930:[13]

The enumeration followed, in general, the 1930, U. S. census definition of a family; namely, that it is a "group of persons, related by either blood or by marriage or adoption, who live together as one household, equally sharing the same table." There are three exceptions to this: first, the Census classes as a lodging house a household with eleven or more lodgers, while here the dividing line is placed at five lodgers; second, the 1930 Census counts two or more related persons occupying permanent quarters in a transient hotel as a family, but they are not so counted here; third, if two families are temporarily living together, "doubling up" as it is called, the Census counts the two families as one, while here they are counted as two.

The first two differences in the methods of enumeration would decrease the number of families in 1934 as compared with those in 1930; the last difference would increase the number of families in 1934. Through this difference in the definition of a family, some idea of the extent of the practice of families living together is brought out. As has been stated, the selected area in Harlem shows an increase of 14.5 percent in the number of families in 1934 over the number in 1930, as compared with seven percent for Manhattan, and twelve percent for the Central Harlem health district.[14] In the selected area of Harlem there were 36,688 families in 1934 and 32,041 in 1930, an increase of 4,647. These statistics indicate that the practice of doubling up in this area is about twice as prevalent as it is generally in Manhattan.

All the data of a nonstatistical character point to overcrowding and the mixing of families among the group in the Harlem area as almost characteristic of the manner of living. Social workers, without exception, report that crowding and doubling up of families among the Puerto Ricans, during all the periods of migration, have been one of the outstanding problems of the group. Like many other groups from tropical countries, the Puerto Ricans have a

[13] *Real Property Inventory*, p. xvi.
[14] See Appendix B.

Housing in New York

fear of the cold. The steam heat offered in practically all of the apartments in the Lower Harlem area is one of the attractions of this district. The Puerto Rican does not want to live in a "cold-water flat" even though it could be obtained at a much cheaper price than the steam-heated apartment. He attempts to pay the high rental of the district by taking in other families or lodgers. This practice of mixing families and taking in lodgers is

Table 19. NUMBER OF FAMILIES ACCORDING TO SIZE BY CENSUS TRACTS OF HARLEM SETTLEMENT

Census tracts	166	168	172	174	182	184	186
Total families	2813	2618	2477	3104	2796	3903	1662
1 to 4 persons	1643	1666	1483	1911	1980	2498	1046
Percent of total	58.4	63.6	59.9	61.6	70.8	64.0	62.9
5 to 8 persons	1075	901	881	1087	740	1284	552
Percent of total	38.2	34.4	35.5	35.0	26.5	32.9	33.3
9 persons and over	95	51	113	106	76	121	64
Percent of total	3.4	2.0	4.6	3.4	2.7	3.1	3.8
Census tracts (cont.)	190	198	200	216	218	220	222
Total families	2541	1123	726	2809	2410	2039	1020
1 to 4 persons	1791	771	593	2118	1748	1604	814
Percent of total	70.5	68.7	81.7	75.4	72.5	78.7	79.8
5 to 8 persons	670	319	125	625	603	394	175
Percent of total	26.4	28.4	17.2	22.2	25.0	19.3	17.2
9 persons and over	80	33	8	66	59	41	31
Percent of total	3.1	2.9	1.1	2.4	2.5	2.0	3.0

not primarily a result of the depression, but has always existed to a pronounced degree. Several years prior to the depression, one large social agency, after an investigation of conditions among the group, described them as follows: "Every available resource is utilized. Sometimes a bed occupied at night by one person is rented to another for the day time hours. It is not a question of renting of rooms, but rather beds, in many cases."[15] In the years prior to the depression, rentals in the area were exceedingly high, and the Puerto Rican attempted to meet them in much the same way as he does at the present time.

THE BROOKLYN AREA

The area in Brooklyn is of much less importance than the one in Harlem. The Puerto Rican population living in this district

[15] Taken from a confidential report of a large New York charity organization.

is probably only about one-fifth as large as that of the one in Lower and East Harlem. The Department of Health of New York City has recently defined the district in Brooklyn in which Puerto Ricans are most numerous as follows: "Along the waterfront, from the Navy Yard south to Gowanus Canal, and extending inland to about Third Avenue."[16] The boundaries of the Brooklyn area, which correspond roughly to those defined above, are as follows (the enumeration of the census tracts will be found in Appendix C):

Beginning at Brooklyn Bridge on East River, East River to Navy Yard, Navy St. to Nassau, Nassau to Portland, Portland to Atlantic Ave., Fourth Ave. to First St., First to Gowanus Bay, Gowanus Bay and Erie Basin, Buttermilk Channel.

A large porportion of the Brooklyn area is a water-front section with a mixture of racial groups. Numerous docks are found on the west and south sides of the area, and the occupation of longshoreman is one of the most important in the community. The southern part of the selected area is an isolated community with a business section on the north and a water front on the other three sides.[17] Like the Harlem area, this section has many different cultural groups. There are numerous Italians and a few Irish. Other groups which have moved into the section are Puerto Ricans, Brazilians, Syrians, and Egyptians. Only about six percent of the entire population living in the area is colored.[18] The Puerto Ricans are comparatively newcomers and constitute one of the smaller racial groups. Their main reason for locating in this particular neighborhood is that it is one of the lowest rental areas available.[19] About one-third of the Puerto Ricans in the Brooklyn settlement are colored as compared with about one-fifth in the district in Lower Harlem.[20] Although the Puerto Rican settlement

[16] *Quarterly Bulletin,* City of New York, Vol. II, No. 4, 1934, p. 79.
[17] A good description of this particular area was given in the study of the Crime Commission of New York State, *A Study of Delinquency in a District of King's County,* by the Sub-Commission, of cause and effect of crime (J. B. Lyon, printers, Albany, 1927), pp. 9 and 10. Many of the worst houses have now been condemned and boarded up.
[18] Based on *Real Property Inventory,* 1934.
[19] Source: charity organizations.
[20] The basis for this statement is shown on p. 63.

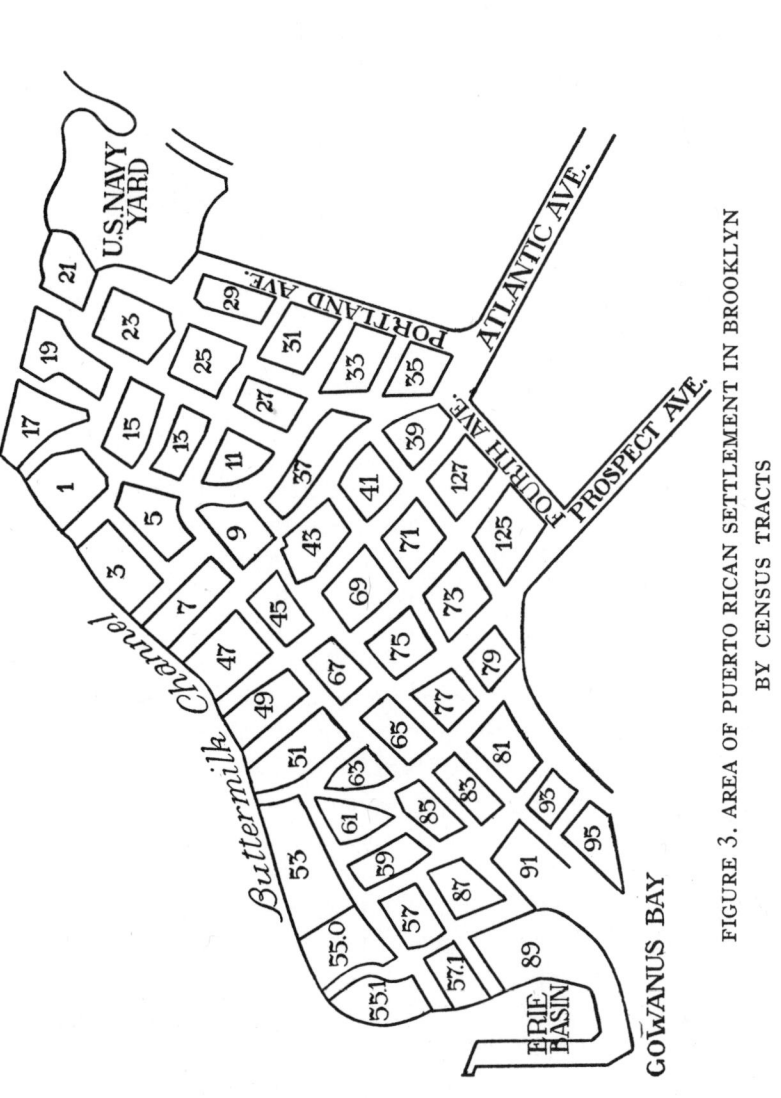

FIGURE 3. AREA OF PUERTO RICAN SETTLEMENT IN BROOKLYN BY CENSUS TRACTS

in this area is scattered, most of the Puerto Ricans will be found in the district adjoining and west of the Navy Yard, and in or near the Italian settlements along the docks. The greatest concentration is in census tracts 13, 15, 17, 19, 21, 23, 25, 47, 49, 51, 53, and 67. The settlement along the docks is approximately in the center of Figure 3 on the west side.

GENERAL CHARACTERISTICS OF HOUSING IN THE BROOKLYN SETTLEMENT

In contrast to the area selected in Harlem, the one in Brooklyn is not nearly so densely populated. Only one census tract in the area is in the highest classification of residential population density, from 200 to 500 persons per acre. A little less than one-third of all the tracts selected fall into the second classification, 100 to 200 persons per acre.[21]

On the whole, the area is one of extremely poor conditions in many respects. (See data given in Appendix B.) Nearly ninety-five percent of all the structures in this area are thirty-five years old, or older; the area has only a few new buildings. In age of buildings, this area presents a less favorable condition than the area selected in Harlem, the Lower East Side, or Central Harlem.

About seventeen percent of the buildings were reported to be in good condition. The proportion in good condition is better than that of the area selected in Harlem, the Lower East Side, or the Central Harlem district. On the other hand, the proportion (eight percent) of buildings which are unfit for use is high. This proportion is a little less than that of the Lower East Side. The proportion of buildings in good repair and the proportion unfit for use bring out the highly mixed character of the area.

In 1934 nearly eighteen per cent of all of the family quarters were vacant. The proportion of vacancies was smaller than the twenty-one percent shown for the Lower East Side.

About ten per cent of the family quarters had mechanical refrigeration. Approximately forty percent had no baths, and a little less than this proportion had no private toilets. Among the sec-

[21] *Real Property Inventory,* Borough of Brooklyn, maps, p. LXXII.

tions selected, only the Lower East Side presents worse conditions.

No important change took place in the total number of families in the area between 1930 and 1934. About thirty-nine percent of the total number of families paid less than twenty dollars per month rental; thirty-three percent paid between twenty and thirty dollars per month; thus, over seventy percent of the total number of families paid less than thirty dollars per month. Such figures indicate low standards. Nearly six percent of the rentals were less than three dollars per room. The largest number of quarters rented for from three to four dollars per room. The area is on the whole comparable to that of the Lower East Side.

The description of the southern part of this area given by the New York State Crime Commission in 1926 still holds true to a large degree.[22] Although some of these old houses along the docks have been condemned, the general unsatisfactory conditions found at that time still exist. At the time of the survey, the Commission found that the houses were very old, that few had baths or toilets, that often the toilets were in the hall or back yard, and that in many instances the housing was wretched. The Navy Yard, itself, has a strong neighborhood influence; the section is generally known as a "poor neighborhood," where there is a considerable amount of prostitution.[23]

SUMMARY AND CONCLUSION

The Puerto Ricans in the Harlem section are provided with poorer housing facilities than many of the other groups in the city. As a whole, these facilities are below the average of Manhattan. In some respects, however, they are better than those found in the Lower East Side and the Central Harlem health districts. The area is one of old structures where there is a definite need for repairs and improvements.

Despite the rather poor facilities provided in many cases, rentals in the area tend to be high. Like all of the Harlem area, the particular section has shown a tendency for high rentals due to con-

[22] *A Study of Delinquency in a District of King's County,* p. 10.
[23] Delinquency is discussed in a following chapter; see p. 134.

gestion, the character of the population, and the fact that at most periods the housing facilities are taxed by the migration of additional people from the South and from the West Indies.

With the Puerto Rican group, it is more often with the standards of occupancy, rather than with the facilities themselves, that any serious objection is to be made. The large family is much more prevalent in this area than in Manhattan. Statistical data also show that the practice of families living together in this area is greater than in other sections. A general agreement exists among people dealing with the Puerto Rican group, whether from the standpoint of health service, public relief, or the private charity organization, that the mixed family and the presence of lodgers in the family constitute unusual problems because of their general prevalence. Not only do these unsatisfactory standards of occupancy exist, but there are other neighborhood factors about which evidence is given in later chapters, such as the incidence of pulmonary tuberculous, venereal disease, and numerous arrests in the area.[24] Poor housing, together with these factors, has caused at least a part of the area to be included in the slum-elimination program of the city.

The character of the housing in the Brooklyn area is less favorable than that of the area in Harlem. Practically all of the buildings are old, and a large proportion of the family quarters do not have baths and private indoor toilets. Unsatisfactory conditions and standards are also indicated by the low rentals paid by the majority of the families.

On account of their poverty, the Puerto Ricans in the Harlem and Brooklyn areas often occupy the more unfavorable quarters. The conditions under which the colored Puerto Rican family lives, especially in the Brooklyn area, are in many cases wretched. Unsanitary conditions are frequently found among these very poor families both in the Harlem and Brooklyn areas.

All of the evidence shows that the average Puerto Rican worker and his family still continue to live under crowded and unsatisfactory conditions in New York. Although general sanitary conditions in New York are vastly better and housing on the whole

[24] See statement of James Ford, *Slums and Housing*, I, 336.

is better than in Puerto Rico, there are important differences. Because of the climate and apartment-house living, the Puerto Rican family is much more confined in New York. Fresh air and sunlight are no longer plentiful as they are on the island. Crowding under these urban conditions where there is a lack of sunlight and air might have more serious consequences in New York than in Puerto Rico. Much of the advantage of New York's improvement in housing facilities for the family of the low-income group, as compared with housing in Puerto Rico, is offset by the changed living conditions in this urban environment.

CHAPTER VII

The Problem of Health

THE MIGRANT from Puerto Rico to New York City is apt to be at a disadvantage as compared with persons of other racial groups on account of the unsatisfactory health conditions on the island. In the brief discussion of some of the health problems existing in Puerto Rico, given in Chapter III, it was shown that the disease which takes the greatest number of lives there each year is tuberculosis, for which the mortality rate, which is over 300 per 100,000 population, is between five and six times that of the United States. Important factors explaining the high death rate from this disease were found in the crowded living conditions, lack of proper facilities for isolation, and the general low economic status of the people. In contrast to the United States, a large proportion of the population is also infested with some form of parasitical disease, such as malaria or hookworm. The very high death rates from diarrhea and enteritis show poverty and lack of proper sanitation. Mortality rates from the principal diseases are much higher than in New York, and general health conditions are distinctly lower. Since there is no medical examination required for people coming from the island to New York, the question naturally arises as to what extent these poor health conditions and susceptibility to certain diseases, such as tuberculosis, prevail among the group in New York.

Equally as important as these unsatisfactory health conditions on the island in explaining the poor health of the Puerto Rican worker in New York is his low standard of living here. Having, as a rule, a low economic status, he settles in a highly congested area and under crowded conditions, where there may be constant and close contact with infected persons. Unemployment, low earnings, poor diet, and other factors affect his ability to resist infection. It has been shown that the worker from the island is often

The Problem of Health

unskilled and without union affiliation in New York, and has difficulty in meeting the conditions of a changed labor market. His wages are generally low and he is often unemployed. Many Puerto Rican families have become dependent upon public relief or some other form of charity. The general practice of doubling up and the necessity for taking in lodgers also have an effect upon the health of the worker and the members of his family.

HEALTH CENTER DISTRICTS

The settlement of the Puerto Rican worker and his family in certain districts in New York City would naturally affect the health conditions in these districts; and the Puerto Rican would, in turn, be affected by the general conditions prevailing in them. Conditions in the districts in which the Puerto Ricans settle are unfavorable as compared with those of other districts and the entire city. A good idea of the conditions prevailing in these areas of settlement will be found from a study of the statistical data of the health center districts of New York City. In Manhattan, the Puerto Rican usually settles in the Central and East Harlem districts; in Brooklyn, in the Red Hook-Gowanus district. Health statistics for these districts show the health conditions under which the Puerto Rican in New York lives. Table 20 presents data for all the districts of Manhattan and Brooklyn, and will serve to emphasize the wide differences in mortality and morbidity rates for the different parts of the city.

Among the Manhattan districts, the Central Harlem district has the highest rate for infant and tuberculosis mortality and for venereal disease registration. It ranks second in the registration of such contagious diseases as measles, whooping cough, and scarlet fever, and third for pneumonia and all causes of death. The East Harlem district also shows high rates for tuberculosis, infant mortality, and the registration of measles, whooping cough, scarlet fever, and venereal diseases. Among the Brooklyn districts, the Red Hook-Gowanus district ranks first in the mortality rate from all causes, pneumonia, tuberculosis, and venereal disease registration. It is second in infant mortality and the registration for measles, whooping cough, and scarlet fever.

112 The Problem of Health

Health conditions in the Puerto Rican settlement and their effect upon the general mortality rates for the city are revealed more specifically in the data given by the Department of Health

Table 20. Mortality Rates and New Case Registration in Manhattan and Brooklyn, 1929-33

District	Mortality Rate				New Case Registration	
	All Causes[a]	Infant[b]	Tuberculosis[c]	Pneumonia[c]	Whooping Cough[d]	Measles, Scarlet Fever, Venereal Diseases[c]
New York City (transients and unknown omitted)	10.32	55	66	116	377	653
Manhattan Districts						
Lower West Side	17.05	75	155	203	762	1,450
Lower East Side	14.89	63	119	191	733	1,097
Central Harlem	14.66	94	247	180	1,089	3,133
Kips Bay-Lenox Hill	12.84	65	71	141	774	862
East Harlem	12.37	77	131	174	1,096	1,115
Riverside	12.19	58	68	128	715	911
Washington Heights	10.24	53	68	99	582	744
Brooklyn Districts						
Red Hook-Gowanus	13.95	71	101	186	403	927
Fort Greene	13.39	74	87	174	460	913
Bushwick	12.11	56	56	129	247	446
Williamsburg-Greenpoint	11.29	66	70	145	259	449
Bedford	10.93	54	53	111	275	458
Sunset Park	9.73	54	52	115	256	352
Flatbush	8.64	40	32	81	261	237
Bay Ridge	7.78	43	34	96	188	289
Brownsville	7.52	51	34	91	130	246
Lower Flatbush	7.47	44	29	92	199	255

Source: Department of Health, New York City, *Health Center Districts*, 1935.
[a] Per 1,000.   [b] Per 1,000 live births.   [c] Per 100,000.
[d] Annual average rate per 100,000 population under 15 years of age, 1930-33.

for health areas.[1] Figure 4 shows the health areas which contain a large Puerto Rican population. The death rate from all causes in all of these areas is much higher than that of the entire city, and generally higher than that of Manhattan. Infant mortality rates for these areas are higher than those for the entire city and for Manhattan. The tuberculosis mortality rates are in every case

[1] A division of the health center district, usually made up of several sanitary districts.

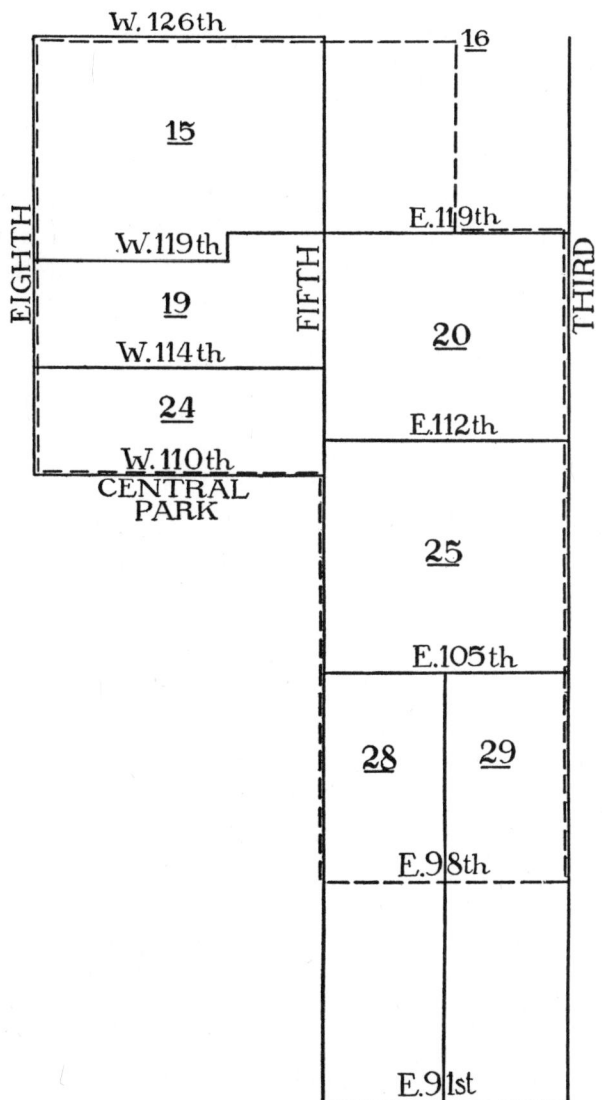

FIGURE 4. MORTALITY RATES OF HARLEM HEALTH AREAS WITH LARGE PUERTO RICAN POPULATION

Source: Department of Health, New York City, "Health Center Districts," 1935. Approximate boundaries of settlement are shown by broken lines.

double the rate for the entire city, and in some areas are almost four times as great. These rates are in most cases nearly twice as high as those for the borough of Manhattan. It is clear from a study of the data given for the areas where there is a large Puerto Rican population that the settlement of the Puerto Rican and other Spanish-speaking people has an effect similar to that caused by the settlement of the colored population in that it increases the general mortality rate and causes a much higher rate for infant and tuberculosis mortality.

Table 21. MORTALITY RATES FOR THE FIVE-YEAR PERIOD 1929–33

Area	All Causes (Per 1,000 Population)	Infant (Per 1,000 Births)	Tuberculosis (Per 100,000 Population
New York City	10.32	55	66
Manhattan	13.41	70	119
Health Area 15	14.88	90	221
Health Area 19	14.00	86	253
Health Area 25	13.94	84	160
Health Area 20	13.76	91	208
Health Area 24	12.28	83	193

The statistical data of the health center district and the health area show the health conditions for all of the racial groups living in the area. The fact that a district such as Central Harlem has serious problems of health is well known, and all three of the districts, Central Harlem, East Harlem, and Red Hook-Gowanus, are classified by the Department of Health as "sore spot" areas. As these statistics do not, however, furnish particular information about the Puerto Rican group, it is now necessary to point out the available information which applies specifically to them.

TUBERCULOSIS AMONG THE PUERTO RICANS IN NEW YORK

Tuberculosis is the outstanding health problem of the Puerto Rican in New York, as on the island. This fact is, of course, related directly to the high prevalence of the disease and mortality rates in Puerto Rico. As has been stated in a previous chapter, mortality rates from tuberculosis in Puerto Rico are as high as, if not higher than, those in any other country in the world for which statistics

The Problem of Health

are available. In 1935, deaths from tuberculosis per 100,000 of population were as follows:[2]

Total island	304.5
Urban	403.0
Rural	253.4

The mortality rates on the island are higher for colored persons than for white, and higher for females than for males:[3]

	Male	Female
White	260.6	307.7
Colored	359.9	374.5

The mortality rates for tuberculosis among the Puerto Rican group in New York appear to be fully as high as on the island. Although based upon small numbers, and therefore perhaps unreliable, the mortality rates per 100,000 population for all forms of tuberculosis for Puerto Ricans living in New York City, for the years 1930 and 1931, were as follows:[4]

	Total	White	Colored
Mortality rate	434	370	663
Average number of deaths annually, 1930-31	195	129	66

The figures given above, if taken without considering the fact that they are based upon these small numbers, would indicate that the mortality rate from tuberculosis among Puerto Ricans living in New York is about one-third higher than that on the island, and about the same as the urban rate of Puerto Rico. From these figures, there also appears to be a terrific mortality rate from this disease among the colored Puerto Ricans, much higher than that among colored persons living on the island. These mortality rates tend to bear out the opinion that the Puerto Ricans, coming from a country where there is a high prevalence of tuberculosis, are forced by their economic situation upon entering this country to live under conditions which afford a ready medium for the transmission of the disease.

The high mortality rates for the people of Puerto Rican origin

[2] Commissioner of Health of Puerto Rico, *Annual Report*, pp. 68 and 69.
[3] *Ibid.*
[4] Data taken from a special study made by G. J. Drolet for the New York Tuberculosis and Health Association.

in New York are brought out clearly by a comparison of their mortality rates with those of other racial groups. Table 22 shows the mortality rates from pulmonary tuberculosis in 1930 and 1931 for the population of New York City, classified according to country of birth.

Table 22. PULMONARY TUBERCULOSIS MORTALITY IN NEW YORK CITY, 1930–31

Country of Birth	Average Mortality Rate[a]	Population[b]	Number of Deaths 1930	Number of Deaths 1931	Annual Average
Puerto Rico (colored)	581	10,152	62	56	59
Puerto Rico (white)	335	34,756	129	104	117
China	581	6,629	27	50	39
Japan	374	1,871	5	9	7
United States (colored)	259	267,783	674	712	693
Ireland	127	220,631	278	282	280
Cuba and other West Indies (colored)	114	48,263	52	58	55
Scandinavia	84	86,493	74	71	72
Austria-Hungary	78	187,052	145	147	146
England	61	78,003	53	42	47
Italy	53	440,250	235	231	233
Russia	50	442,431	232	212	222
Cuba and other West Indies (white)	50	13,032	6	7	7
Germany	45	237,588	107	107	107
United States (white)	44	4,259,069	1,945	1,839	1,892
Poland	42	238,339	94	106	100
Other countries	95	358,104	339	337	338
Total		6,930,446	4,457	4,370	

Source: Special tabulation made by G. J. Drolet for the New York Tuberculosis and Health Association, based on data given in *Weekly Bulletin* of the Department of Health, City of New York, October 8, 1932.

[a] Number of deaths per 100,000 persons.

[b] Persons born in the United States include 8,219 persons born in outlying possessions other than Puerto Rico. The number shown under "other countries" includes 2,152 Mexicans. Some of these rates are based upon small numbers and are, therefore, subject to unreliability.

The prevalence of tuberculosis among the Puerto Ricans in New York is also shown by the X-ray examinations conducted by the Department of Health of New York City. The results of the examination of 7,140 persons are shown in Table 23.[5] All of the in-

---

[5] The conclusion drawn by the Department of Health from the data given in Table 23 was that important cases of tuberculosis were much more prevalent among the Puerto Ricans than among the whites and colored, and that the same condition prevailed regarding suspected cases of tuberculosis. The reader will note that the

dividuals examined were drawn from relief lists in the areas where there were large settlements of Negroes and Puerto Ricans. It was stated by those making the examination that so great a proportion of the population in these areas was on relief that a group drawn from relief lists was probably fairly representative. There is no reason to believe that one group was favored in the selection as compared with others, and persons were not selected because of any previous indication of the disease.

Table 23. X-RAY DIAGNOSES OF 7,140 INDIVIDUALS IN HARLEM

Diagnoses	Percent			Number		
	White	Colored	Puerto Rican	White	Colored	Puerto Rican
Total X-rayed				2,505	3,897	738
Negative diagnoses	81.8	78.5	79.9	2,048	3,059	590
Positive diagnoses needing no investigation	5.3	4.4	5.7	134	170	42
Positive diagnoses to be investigated:						
Important tuberculosis	2.2	2.0	3.2	56	79	24
Tuberculosis suspects	4.3	4.6	5.9	106	177	43
Healed lesions						
Tuberculous	1.8	1.45	1.6	46	56	12
Nontuberculous	—	.05	—	1	2	0
Etiology unknown	1.1	.7	.3	28	28	2
Heart condition	3.4	8.4	3.4	86	326	25

Source: Department of Health, New York City, "Health Problems among Puerto Ricans in New York City," 1934 (unpublished).

Figure 5 shows the tabulation by percent of a total of 10,173 persons who had been examined in Harlem by X-ray, in 1933, and found to have tuberculosis. It will be noted that this table shows the number in each group which was X-rayed. These results show the need of early and intensive work on tuberculosis in these areas.

In July of 1935, the Department of Health established a case-finding program for Puerto Ricans at the Meinhard Clinic, 130 East 101st Street, and the work has continued up to the present time. During the period from the establishment of the program

percentages given in the table are based upon small numbers and also upon an unequal number of cases, which would affect their comparability.

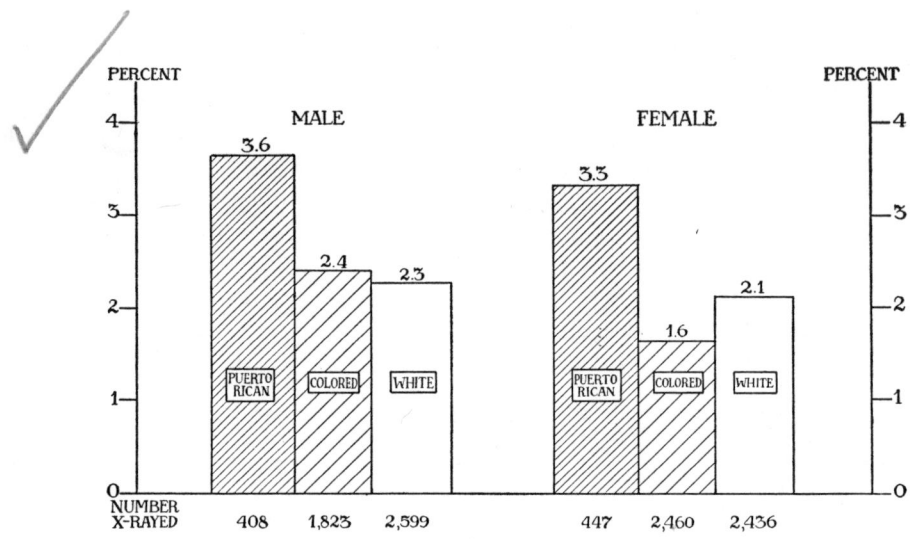

FIGURE 5. PERCENT OF 10,178 PERSONS IN HARLEM FOUND BY X-RAY TO HAVE TUBERCULOSIS, NEW YORK CITY, 1933

Source: Department of Health, New York City, "Health Problems among Puerto Ricans in New York City," 1934. These are adjusted percents obtained by applying the percent for each age group to the age distribution of the combined white, colored, and Puerto Rican populations X-rayed.

The Problem of Health

to December, 1936, 3,768 were examined; 244 had tuberculosis, and 78 of this number had the disease in the active stage. It was also discovered that from seventy to eighty percent of the diseased were then in the minimal stage. The individuals included in this survey were drawn from relief rolls and were not selected because of any knowledge of tuberculosis history or symptoms.[6] It was the opinion of those making the examination that the figures were very significant in that this amount of tuberculosis was found among apparently well individuals. It is also significant that so great a percentage of the cases were found to be in the initial stages of the disease.

There is at the present time no assembled data to show whether the prevalence of tuberculosis among the Puerto Ricans in New York is increasing or decreasing. The results of recent X-ray examinations made by the Department of Health have not been tabulated, and mortality rates for specific groups cannot be accurately determined until the census of 1940.

The problem of tuberculosis in a racial group, to the extent to which it exists among the Puerto Ricans at least, is related to the adequacy of the facilities of the city for treatment and segregation. Since the facilities of the Department of Health are extended freely to all persons, without discrimination, it cannot be said that these facilities in New York are any more inadequate for the Puerto Rican than for any other citizen. In 1937, the Department of Health of the city of New York had about as many hospital beds as there were deaths from tuberculosis in the city during the year. This number is considered by health authorities to be entirely too low, and it is stated that the minimum requirement should be one and one-half times as many beds as there are deaths annually from the disease.[7] This shortage of beds limits the ability of the department to institute bed or surgical treatment promptly for all known cases. For this reason and due to the density of population and overcrowding in family quarters, it is often difficult to break dangerous contacts that exist. This inadequacy of facilities might easily become more serious if there is a very large migration from the island during the next few years.

[6] Data furnished by the Department of Health of New York City.
[7] Data secured from the Department of Health of New York City.

The degree to which tuberculosis is found among the Puerto Ricans in New York is highly significant. Like the infant mortality rate, tuberculosis is rather a sensitive barometer of the general health condition of a given racial group. It has been shown that other diseases, such as scarlet fever, measles, and pneumonia follow practically the same variations according to districts and areas of a city as that of tuberculosis.[8] Tuberculosis, often spoken of as an economic disease, is directly related to the standard of living. With a group of people such as that of the Puerto Ricans in New York, there are many factors of varying significance which might explain the high prevalence of the disease. The change in climate is one factor of importance. Comparatively higher mortality rates from the disease might be expected from any group which has changed its environment from a tropical island to New York City. The main factors entering into the explanation of the existence of the disease and the high mortality rates among the group here would be the fact that so many Puerto Ricans are infected before they leave the island and the fact that in New York they continue to live under extremely crowded conditions, so that the disease rapidly spreads among these people whose poor economic status gives them insufficient vitality to resist it.

PARASITICAL DISEASES

The presence of parasitical diseases in a large proportion of the group constitutes another health problem connected with the migration. It would be expected that people from Puerto Rico would have these diseases since in some localities on the island a majority of the population is infested with one or more parasites. Diseases commonly found among the Puerto Ricans in New York are: the dysenteries, malaria, filariasis, and various worm infestations such as hookworm, ascaris, tapeworm, pinworm, and schistosoma mansoni. As is well known, amoebic dysentery is a very serious disease which may result in invalidism or death, and is much more common in tropical than in temperate climates. Contaminated water is usually the source of this disease. The

[8] This conclusion was based on a series of charts of the Department of Health of New York City. See L. R. Williams, *Tuberculosis*, pp. 67-68.

The Problem of Health 121

bacillary type is sometimes fatal to children or old people. Dysentery is one of the diseases which may be spread by "carriers." Malaria and hookworm are, of course, still common in the southern part of the United States. Hookworm is known to be especially detrimental to children, causing them to be undersized, thin, pale, and backward in their school work. In adults, both of these diseases greatly affect the capacity for work, and often cause a condition described as a lack of ambition. Filariasis is caused by a very small worm which lives in the lymphatics of the body. It is conveyed from one person to another by the bite of a mosquito. Once contracted, the disease may last indefinitely, and it is doubtful that a satisfactory treatment has been found for it. Schistomiasis is not so common, but may cause suffering and disability. The life cycle of the parasite of this disease is dependent upon the snail. Another disease sometimes found is sprue, a chronic diarrhea. The treatment of this disease is the work of the trained specialist, and its cause is not definitely known. It often results in invalidism or death. All of the other worm infestations are at least detrimental to health.[9]

Medical authorities are beginning to stress the importance of these diseases. Dr. F. W. O'Connor of the Department of Medicine, Presbyterian Hospital, Columbia University, in speaking of the problem of parasitical diseases caused by migration from the various countries, commented as follows:[10]

> The Puerto Ricans offer a special problem. They are heavily infested with parasites, which, by causing serious invaliding, interfere with their economic progress. Hookworm, ascaris, and malaria are common among them and a number have schistosoma infection of the liver and intestines, while many have come to this cooler country to avoid the frequently recurring attacks of filarial lymphangitis which are common in their own country.

The Department of Health of New York City is of the opinion that the poor health conditions among the group may be largely due to

[9] Pan American Sanitary Bureau, *Health Suggestions for Travelers in the Americas*, Publication No. 96, Aug., 1934 (written by Bolivar J. Lloyd, Medical Director, U. S. Public Health Service), gives a short description of all of these diseases for the layman.

[10] "Animal Parasitism in Connecticut and Adjoining States," *Yale Journal of Biology and Medicine*, July, 1936, pp. 619-35.

the presence of these parasites. It states that a large proportion of the group examined by various clinics have been found to be suffering from these parasites, and calls attention to the severe disablement caused by some of the diseases.[11]

Further recognition of the problem of these diseases is evidenced by the establishment of special facilities in the Puerto Rican settlement. At the Meinhard Memorial Health Center, at 130 East 101st Street, the Department of Health has created a laboratory with trained technicians who have been accumulating data for several years.[12] Other large hospitals coming in contact with the group are also doing special work in this field.

These parasitical diseases are important for two reasons: first, the suffering and economic loss to the individual; and second, the possible danger of their spreading. Often the infestation is so debilitating that the person is incapable of working, and for this reason finds a serious handicap in his fight for any sort of economic security. The diseases are especially important in children. If a large proportion of the children coming from the island are infested, poor health and lack of progress in school might be expected to follow. Discussion of the danger of the spreading of these diseases is not a task for the layman. Where the presence of the mosquito or snail is required in the life cycle of the parasite, there appears to be little danger in New York. The case is probably not quite so clear if the disease may be spread by means of polluted soil. Evidence is accumulating to show that many of the diseases may be spread in certain ways not clearly understood at the present time. For example, it is now known that an ailment such as hookworm, usually caused by penetration of the parasite through the skin of the foot, may be contracted by mouth, and that this means of contracting the disease is not rare or exceptional.[13] Dogs and cats have received attention as possible sources of parasitical infestation. Unsanitary home conditions, the possibility of contamination in water and food, the use of raw vegetables, and many other factors are also being studied as possible explanations of cases of infestation. One reason why the task is so difficult

[11] John L. Rice, *op. cit.*, p. 6.
[12] Statistics collected up to the present time were not made available to the author.
[13] Information supplied by U. S. Public Health Service.

is that many families are constantly moving from the island to New York to live with people who are already here, and many others are visiting their former homes each year. Diseases of this classification which could be spread by "carriers" would be of special importance because of the rather large number of Puerto Ricans who are employed in domestic, hotel, and restaurant work.

GENERAL HEALTH CONDITIONS AMONG THE GROUP

All clinics and hospitals which serve large numbers of Puerto Rican patients in New York City agree that general health conditions among them are poor.[14] There also appears to be a general lack of coöperation on the part of Puerto Ricans with medical authorities concerning personal and community health problems; this may be due in part to the language difficulty. The highest infant mortality rates are found in areas in which there are a large number of people from Puerto Rico.[15] Although these areas are at the present time served by baby health stations and prenatal clinics, there is still a need for increased facilities to care properly for all of the people in the district. In 1929 a special study was made of the general health problem of the Puerto Rican in New York by the out-patient department of one of the large hospitals. This report found the diseases most prevalent among them to be tuberculosis, syphilis, malnutrition, and fevers of unknown origin. It also stated that they often did not realize the seriousness of their illnesses, that they were ignorant of hygiene and sanitation, and that only a small percentage were coöperative. The large majority of the children were reported to be undernourished, and it was said to be difficult to obtain necessary information about their cases because they were usually brought to the hospital by neighbors, relatives, or boarders. Attention was also called to the danger to the community from congested living quarters and the fact that children were often exposed to the last stages of tuberculosis and other diseases.[16]

[14] John L. Rice, op. cit., p. 5.
[15] Based on statement of the Department of Health. No specific infant mortality statistics are yet available for the Puerto Rican group in New York.
[16] This report was submitted to the Welfare Council for study by its committee.

Puerto Ricans in New York City often suffer from venereal diseases. There is a common belief that these diseases are more prevalent in all of the West Indies than in the United States.[17] This idea, like the one that syphilis originated in the West Indies, could probably not be supported by statistical data. The Department of Health has recently instituted a program in the Harlem district for the treatment of one thousand cases of venereal disease per week. Concerning the Puerto Ricans, it makes the following comment:[18]

During the three-year period, 1931-33, an average of 6,231 new cases of syphilis were reported annually in Central Harlem and 2,137 in East Harlem. This is at the rate of 3,056 per 100,000 population in Central Harlem and 1,010 in East Harlem compared with a rate of 552 for the city as a whole. It is the opinion of workers in this field that the Puerto Rican population contributes a large share of this case load.

THE PROBLEM OF DIET

The securing of proper nutrition is a problem directly connected with that of health. In Puerto Rico it is often said that the man of the poorer economic class is striving to secure calories rather than vitamins. Malnutrition is common among people of the low-income group on the island. New York nutritionists criticize the Puerto Rican diet and point out that it lacks calories, that it is low in essential minerals—particularly calcium—and that it is especially deficient in vitamin content, particularly vitamins A and D.[19] Rice and beans are the main articles of food of the poorer classes. Beans are their chief source of protein. There are few green or leafy vegetables. Milk and eggs are rarely used by the poorer families. Bread is not generally used in all parts of the island. Dried and salt fish make up a small part of the food consumed. Since so much of the food contains starch, the Puerto Rican adds cheap fats—

---

[17] "Conditions [in Puerto Rico] are perhaps rather loosely reported to be similar to those in the British West Indian Islands, where, according to a recent report, a very considerable percentage of the population is infected with hereditary or contracted syphilis."—Clark, *op. cit.*, p. 66.

[18] John L. Rice, *op. cit.*, p. 5.

[19] Data concerning diet is largely from a mimeographed study, "The Porto Rican Diet," prepared by New York nutritionists for the use of social workers (Luise Draus Addiss, Charity Organization Society, Chairman, 1930).

The Problem of Health

usually lard or olive oil—in liberal quantities.[20] Very often indigestion and intestinal disorders result from a diet with too much grease. Puerto Ricans drink coffee in large quantities, and children begin its use at the time they are weaned. Puerto Rican mothers in New York have to be taught the use of fresh cow's milk for their children, and the children have to cultivate a taste for it. Baking and other forms of cooking should be substituted for the general practice of frying. Children in Puerto Rico, while they are often pale and anemic, do not have rickets in the same form as is found in the United States, on account of the abundant sunshine. The need for cod-liver oil in New York to make up for the deficiency of sunshine is not generally appreciated by Puerto Rican mothers. The Puerto Rican worker should add milk and other dairy products, as well as fresh vegetables, inexpensive fresh fish, and dried fruits, to his diet. Although the Puerto Rican, as a rule, does not like American food, it is important for him to realize that there is a great difference in the kind of food required in a northern climate where strong and abundant sunshine is not available. Because of this fact, diet and proper nutrition form an important part of a health program among the group.

A problem similar to that of diet results from the fact that the women of the island in particular do not understand the necessity for warm clothing in the New York climate. Until Spanish-speaking nurses were employed in the Harlem clinics during the last few years, Puerto Rican mothers were often unable to profit from the advice of physicians about the use of warm clothing for themselves and for their children. As a result, the Puerto Rican family often suffered from exposure and respiratory diseases.

SUMMARY

The health of the Puerto Rican worker and his family in New York shows no great improvement over that in Puerto Rico. Mortality rates from tuberculosis appear to be fully as high as those found on the island. For the colored Puerto Rican, tuberculosis is much worse here than on the island. The danger of transmission

---

[20] The use of generous amounts of olive oil and other grease in cooking is not confined to Puerto Rico; it is a characteristic of Spanish cooking as well.

of this disease may be fully as great in New York as in Puerto Rico. Here, the migrants are usually crowded together with other families. Urban dwellings deprive them of sunshine and air. Instead of the small frame houses found in Puerto Rico, they now live in steam-heated apartments. The strong rays of the tropical sun of their native island no longer penetrate all parts of their dwellings each day.

A large proportion of the group here continue to suffer from parasitical diseases. The presence of these diseases usually causes suffering, serious economic loss, and also a possible danger of infection to others.

From the standpoint of the community, the settlement of the Puerto Rican is similar to that of the Negro migration in that it has increased mortality rates and created health problems. The prevalence of tuberculosis is much greater among the Puerto Ricans then among the colored groups, and they present a special problem on account of parasitical diseases. Community medical service is far better in New York than in Puerto Rico. In New York the Puerto Rican of the low-income group finds greater specialization, better facilities, and a larger variety of medical services furnished by the community. There are also excellent facilities and medical staffs which have been created especially for him. Because of the worker's low economic status, the crowded conditions under which he lives, and the low health standards prevailing on the island, a large migration to New York in the near future would necessitate increased facilities, further specialization in tropical diseases, and greater appropriations for medical care.

CHAPTER VIII

Social Adjustment in the New Community

THIS chapter attempts to show with what degree of success the Puerto Rican worker has been able to meet some of the problems of social adjustment in the new community. It takes up crime and delinquency as evidence of social maladjustment, the problem of family disintegration arising out of the migration, the attempt being made by the migrant to secure a better preparation for work, recreation and social activities in the Harlem settlement, and the worker's reaction to religious and political influences.

The communities in which the Puerto Ricans settle, which constitute one of the most important environmental influences affecting the worker and his family, have already been described in preceding chapters. Since the discussion of social adjustment deals for the most part with the group of migrants living in Lower and East Harlem, where the majority of them settle, a few more details about these sections of the city are necessary to picture more clearly the influences and the life found in them.

A CLOSER VIEW OF THE HARLEM SETTLEMENT OF PUERTO RICANS

The East Harlem settlement is, in all respects, a slum area where all of the social problems arising out of extreme poverty, deplorable housing, and other unfavorable influences exist. On account of cheaper rentals, there has always been a tendency for a large number of the colored Puerto Ricans to live in this area. The conditions of the Puerto Rican group in this section are among the worst to be found in New York. As there are few parks or playgrounds in the neighborhood, during the summer months the children of all the groups living in the area swarm into the streets. Sidewalk are frequently blocked by games of cards or craps in which youths who have almost reached maturity are taking part. The community has only a few places of commercial amusement. Some of the need for wholesome recreation is met by such agencies as the Union Settlement, a community settlement house, located on East 104th Street. Except for a number of small grocery stores and a few barber shops and pool rooms, there is comparatively little business in the area. In these little grocery stores, the trade is slow and often the customer buys only ten or fifteen cents worth of food. Because of its poverty, its lack of institutions and places of entertainment, and its inability to support business enterprises, the East Harlem settlement is regarded by the Puerto Ricans as decidedly less favorable than the one near 116th Street, and many of its residents hope to leave it and move to Lower Harlem as soon as they can do so.

The largest concentration of Puerto Ricans and other Spanish-speaking people, as already shown, is found up Madison Avenue from the East Harlem settlement at about 115th or 116th Streets. As shown in a preceding chapter, a great variety of housing conditions exist in this area, but on the whole they are less favorable than those of the city generally. There is an absence of railroad yards, tracks, coal yards, and docks or other large structures which so often influence behavior unfavorably. Another favorable influence is the proximity of parks. Central Park forms the general southern boundary of the area; Mount Morris Park marks the approximate extension to the north; and the high precipices of Morningside Park form a sort of natural boundary on the west.

In this settlement are almost all of the important institutions and places of business which serve the Puerto Rican people in New York. As in the East Harlem settlement, the most common type of business is the small grocery store. There are also a number of barber shops, drug stores, and other shops, as well as pool rooms, bars, and political clubs. One important Puerto Rican institution in this neighborhood is the employment office which has already been referred to. At 103 West 110th Street is the Puerto Rican Service Center of New York. This organization, while yet young and doing only a small amount of case work, often intercedes for the unfortunate Puerto Rican family with charity organizations or relief agencies. Near the boundary of the settlement on Fifth Avenue are such institutions as the Heckscher Foundation for Children and the Fifth Avenue Hospital. Practically all of the large charity, recreational, and health agencies serve this community through branch offices in or near it. On 114th Street and Seventh Avenue is the beautiful Catholic Church for Spanish-speaking people, Nuestra Señora de la Medalla Milagrosa. There are many small churches of other faiths. Some of the Protestant churches are located on the second floor of various types of buildings, and as one approaches Upper Harlem there is a tendency for them to become more numerous. There are also some important places of amusement for the Puerto Rican group in this settlement. At the northeast corner of Central Park, at 110th Street, is El Toreador, called in its radio programs a Spanish-American night club. Its prices are high for the working man, but there is real Spanish dancing and music. All of the well-known Spanish eating places in New York, which are often of the night-club variety, are located outside of the settlement. The Cervantes is one of the largest moving picture theaters in the settlement, and the Teatro Hispano, a smaller theater, usually combines moving pictures with Spanish musical acts and other entertainment.

La Prensa has been for many years the daily newspaper of the Spanish-speaking people in New York. This paper contains not only news about the Puerto Ricans in New York but also a considerable number of reports from the island. Many other publications in Spanish have appeared from time to time, but this paper seems to be the only one which has lasted without interruption for many years. The issue of the war in Spain brought into existence a new daily tabloid paper, *La Voz,* which is now generally sold at newsstands over the city. A Communistic paper published in Spanish is occasionally distributed in Harlem by those interested in this movement.

The community has, to a large degree, taken on the color and customs of the Spanish-speaking countries. In certain sections Spanish is generally spoken. Some of the stores have no signs in English at all, and seem to depend entirely upon Spanish-speaking customers. The newly arrived Puerto Rican may, at least for the moment, feel very much at home as he hears the strains of "Besos, muchos besos," a popular song on the island, coming from music stores, or smells the odor of roast pig—a delicacy in all of the West Indies. Talking and visiting are important pastimes, and Fascist aid to Franco is a favorite topic of street-corner conversation at the present time. Numerous unemployed men loiter about the streets or in pool rooms. Even the loud noises which are so characteristic of Puerto Rico are not entirely lacking. Due to the large number of Spanish-speaking people in this community, and to these customs and characteristics, it has been called "Little Spain."

As in East Harlem, although probably not to the same degree, the poverty of the people is a characteristic of the community. One evidence of this is the frequency with which the sign "Cuarto privado," or room for rent, appears in the windows of the homes. This would bear out the fact that a large number of the families take lodgers into their homes to help pay their rent. Although some of the residents show plainly the effects of poverty, there is little begging or "panhandling" on the streets. A good idea of the plight of many of the people living here can be obtained by visiting the large home-relief agency, located on Madison Avenue in what is practically the center of the colony. Many demonstrations or relief strikes have taken place from time to time in front of this building. Inside of this office, thirty-five or forty people are usually sitting on benches waiting for their names to be called.

The entire settlement seems to take on an increased activity at night. There are many people on the streets, Spanish music can be heard from the music and radio shops, dances are in progress, and the bars and restaurants are prosperous. The Puerto Rican, if not attending some social gathering, may find entertainment and conversation at the home of a friend. Those not so fortunate as to be invited to some home can always find friends on the streets. Seldom is it necessary for a Puerto Rican to leave the section in order to find entertainment. Few people other than the residents seem to come into the area at night, as New Yorkers who frequent Harlem in "late parties" usually go farther uptown.

This district is not, however, without the same social problems which exist in all of Harlem. Police in the neighborhood report that such offenses as robbery, housebreaking, and prostitution are of frequent occurrance. Although the majority of the residents of any community are probably thoroughly law-abiding, there does exist, according to the residents themselves, a vicious element which may assault or rob those who venture into some of the less-frequented streets at night.

In spite of the fact that Puerto Ricans and other Spanish-speaking people have been able to form a community in which thousands of their group live, and therefore are able to continue, to a large extent, the customs of the island, the migrant encounters a serious problem of social adjustment in this community.

SOCIAL MALADJUSTMENT—CRIME AND DELINQUENCY IN THE COMMUNITY AND AMONG THE GROUP

Court statistics of arrests and convictions show that the sections in which the Puerto Ricans settle have high crime and delinquency rates.[1] Statistical data showing the relation of the slum and crime, given in the recent work of Halpern and his associates, show the records of the court for so-called "slum areas."[2] Of the nine areas selected in Manhattan, having a population of 894,610, a total of 34,375 offenses were reported; in the remaining part of the borough (having a population of 972,702) 25,357 offenses were

[1] It is generally recognized by sociologists that the use of court records to measure crime and delinquency is subject to serious limitations. A recent and valuable contribution on this subject may be found in the work of Sophia M. Robison, *Can Delinquency Be Measured?* This author shows that such statistics may be influenced by the fact that a larger proportion of the delinquent children of one cultural group may be brought into the Children's Court or to other official agencies than that of other groups. (See p. 71.) It is also well-known that attitudes, relations in the family, occupations, and such factors as the amount of police protection, as well as the attitude in making arrests, could easily influence the delinquency rates of the various racial groups or the communities in which they live. Until more accurate and scientific measures are worked out, the records of the courts represent practically the only means available for judging the character of a neighborhood, and their use has been given rather wide sanction as a measure of crime. For example, the Children's Bureau of the U. S. Department of Labor publishes juvenile court statistics. The well-known study of Clifford R. Shaw, *Delinquency Areas* (University of Chicago Press, 1929), relates delinquency petitions to population. See also the various studies of the Crime Commission of New York State. A legal definition of delinquency may be found in the reports of the Children's Court of New York which quotes the laws (Ch. 254, Laws of 1924, as amended to February 1, 1926) of the State of New York.

[2] The character of this study, *Slum and Crime*, was mentioned on p. 91.

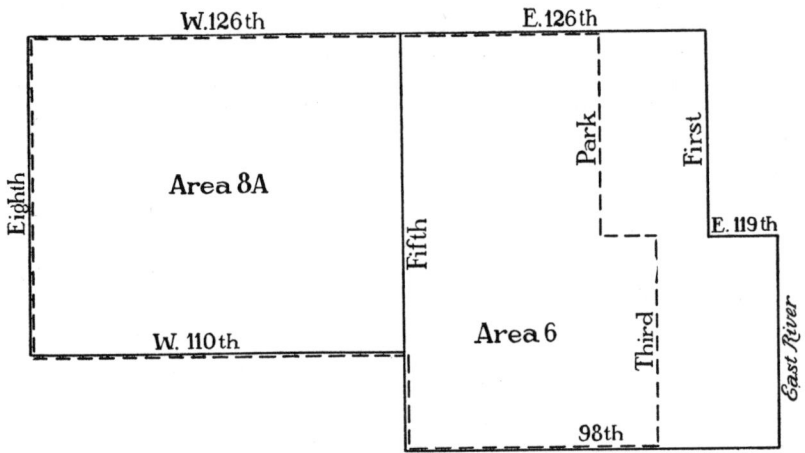

FIGURE 6. AREAS 8A AND 6 OF HALPERN STUDY OF CRIME

Approximate boundaries of Puerto Rican settlement are shown by broken lines.

reported. The total number of juvenile delinquents in these areas was 1,375, as compared with 591 for the remainder of Manhattan. More offenses of all classifications were committed in these areas than in the remainder of the borough. Of the nine areas selected in Manhattan, the areas in this study which are called 8A and 6 correspond roughly to the section in Harlem which has already been discussed as the one which has the largest Puerto Rican population. The boundaries of these two areas are as follows:[3] 8A—West 126th Street to West 110th Street, and Fifth Avenue to Eighth Avenue; 6—East 126th and East 119th Streets to 98th Street, East River to Fifth Avenue.

The part of Harlem which is most predominantly Negro is known in this study as Area 8, and is bounded as follows: West 150th to West 126th Street, Harlem River to Eighth Avenue. Other areas used in the study were defined as follows: 1—West 74th Street to West 42nd Street, Central Park West and Eighth Avenue to Hudson River; 2—West 14th Street and West 11th Street to Canal Street, Waverly Place and Broadway to Hudson River; 3—East Third to East Fifth to New Chambers Street, East River to Bowery; 4—East 24th Street to East Third Street, East River to Third Avenue; 5—East 79th Street to East 59th Street, East River to Third Avenue; 7—East 119th Street to Harlem River, First Avenue to East River.

The authors drew the following conclusions about the number of offenses in these so-called "slum areas":[4]

> Four Manhattan areas contain the densest offender concentrations. . . . They are Areas 6 and 8 in Harlem, and 3 and 4 on the Lower East Side. . . . Areas 6 or 8, both in Harlem, it will be noted, lead in all but one, the petty offender group. In that, Area 3 assumes first place. The most juvenile delinquents resided in Area 6 which also had the third highest number of arrests, and ranks second in petty offenders and misdemeanants. Significantly, Area 1, which borders on the so-called "Great White Way" district, ranks second in female offender frequency.

When the offenders are computed per 1,000 population, Area 6 ranks third in juvenile delinquency, fourth in female offenders, fifth in misdemeanants and felons, and sixth in the number of

[3] *Ibid.*, p. 46.   [4] *Ibid.*, pp. 55-56.

arrests and petty offenders. Area 8A ranks second in felons and misdemeanants, third in the number of arrests and female offenders, fourth in juvenile delinquency, and seventh in petty offenses. According to these figures, this area is one in which crimes of a serious nature are prevalent. Area 8, which represents Upper Harlem, ranks first in all of these classifications except that of petty offenders.

The authors also made a computation of the number of offenses per square block. Their conclusion regarding Area 8A is as follows:[5]

Area 8A is projected into prominence by the computations shown above. It is the tract selected for illustrative purposes in this survey, the findings of which bear out the viewpoint that it is a severe delinquency area. In offender ratio to the square block, area 8A leads in the felon and petty, is second in the arrest, female and misdemeanant groups, and fifth in juvenile delinquents.

The environmental influences of the Brooklyn area in which the Puerto Ricans have settled are also distinctly unfavorable from the standpoint of behavior. The influence of the water-front and sea industries, the wretched housing, the irregular work of the longshoreman, and the mixture of racial groups have already been pointed out. There is a lack of proper sanitation and there are few parks or playgrounds. From all standpoints this area is even less desirable than East Harlem as a home for an immigrant group.

In Brooklyn, one area of the Halpern study included the section near the Navy Yard, or what was called in the study Area 9. It was found that among five slum areas of Brooklyn, Area 9 led in the number of offenders per thousand population for female offenders, misdemeanants, and felons. It held second place among these Brooklyn areas in the number of arrests and in juvenile delinquency. The number of female offenders was especially high in this section, being a median of 7.47 per thousand population as compared with 3.68 for the Manhattan slum areas, 2.05 for the Brooklyn areas, and 8.91 for Area 8 in Manhattan.

Another study dealing with a particular area in Brooklyn in which Puerto Ricans have settled was made by the Crime Com-

[5] *Ibid.*

Social Adjustment 135

mission of New York State in 1927. The area selected covered what is known as Statistical Area K3.[6] This area includes approximately the southern half of the area selected for the study of housing in Brooklyn, and Puerto Ricans were shown to be one racial group living in the section. The physical environment has changed but little since the time of the survey; and it is believed that the same influences which affected behavior at that time still exist. Few new buildings have been constructed in the area; few other changes have been made. This area was selected by the Commission for a study of delinquency because of its very high record of offenses. Here, the Commission found conditions almost uniformly bad. In addition to poor housing and unsanitary conditions, the Commission reported that there was an "utter inadequacy of wholesome community recreation facilities."[7] Many of the boys who were nominally members of churches did not attend. A total of seventy-nine gangs were discovered in the neighborhood. The comment of the Commission on delinquency at that time was as follows:[8]

Two hundred and seventeen cases of boys and girls accused of delinquent acts came to the Brooklyn Children's Court from this section in 1926, or 9 per cent of the total for Brooklyn. Thirty additional girls were held as material witnesses. Six hundred and fifty-eight additional cases were referred during 1926 to Police Welfare Lieutenants in two precincts for supervision. On the average one in every twenty boys between the ages of 5 and 16 had a complaint lodged against him in the Children's Court or the Police Welfare Department in 1926.

These studies bring out a fact that is generally well known; namely, that the areas of settlement of the Puerto Rican, if judged by court records of crime and delinquency, are areas in which there is a high amount of antisocial behavior.

These figures do not, however, show to what extent there is a problem of behavior among the Puerto Ricans. Since Puerto Ricans constitute an important group in such a community as Harlem, there is, of course, an implication that they are responsi-

---

[6] See boundaries, p. 63. Approximately the southern half of area shown in Figure 3, p. 105.
[7] *A Study of Delinquency in a District of King's County,* p. 52.
[8] *Ibid.,* p. 53.

ble for a part of the behavior reflected by the statistics for that particular section.

Although few studies give statistics of crime for racial groups, in one study of juvenile delinquency the figures for the Puerto Rican population have been segregated. Table 24 shows the classification of 10,374 delinquents[9] found in New York City in 1930 according to cultural group.

Table 24. CHILDREN REFERRED AS DELINQUENT IN NEW YORK CITY IN 1930

Birthplace of Parent	Number of Delinquents
Continental United States	2,927
Italy	2,583
Russia	1,606
Poland	625
Austria-Hungary	449
Ireland	353
British West Indies	165
Puerto Rico	144
Greece	101
Norway, Sweden, Denmark	66
Syria	29
Other countries	733
Not reported	593
Total	10,374

Source: Sophia M. Robison, *Can Delinquency Be Measured?* Table 58, p. 234.

If the number of delinquents as shown in Table 24 is compared with the total number of each nationality in 1930 as shown by the census, certain groups, especially the Italian, will be seen to have much higher ratios of delinquency than others. There were 44,908 persons born in Puerto Rico living in New York City in 1930, which constituted .65 of one percent of the total population. Children referred as delinquents and having a parent who was born in Puerto Rico made up 1.4 percent of the total number of

[9] This figure of 10,374 includes both the number derived from the operation of the Children's Court (7,090), official agencies other than Children's Court (2,116), unofficial agencies (828), and mental clinics (340). "In the delinquency count the child is classified as belonging to a family of foreign origin if either the father or the mother was born abroad, with preference given to the father. In those instances in which the father was born in the United States and the mother was born abroad, the child is considered as belonging to the cultural group indicated by the mother's birthplace." (See pp. 176-78.)

delinquents. In Manhattan, persons born in Puerto Rico constituted 1.86 percent of the population, and the percentage of delinquents having a parent who was born in Puerto Rico was 2.8 percent. The fact that the percentage of delinquents among the Puerto Rican group was slightly above that of the group in the total population is not significant. Considering the fact that most Puerto Ricans settle in the Harlem section and the Navy Yard section of Brooklyn, the figures may signify the absence of a serious problem of behavior among Puerto Rican children rather than the existence of one.

Delinquents having a parent who was born in Puerto Rico were concentrated in certain health areas. In Manhattan these areas were 19, 20, 24, and 25, and in Brooklyn, areas 10 and 40.[10] In the health areas named, 92, or about 64 percent, of the Puerto Rican children referred as delinquents were found. In these areas a total of 493 children were referred to agencies as delinquents. Out of this number, 102 of the children had a parent who was born in the continental United States, 128 in Italy, 92 in Puerto Rico, 30 in the British West Indies, 23 in Russia, small numbers in other countries, and 35 not reported. Of the total number classified as delinquent, Puerto Rican children constituted 18.7 percent.

No special problem of serious delinquency is revealed by the analysis of the nature of the offenses of these particular delinquents. See Table 25, which appears on the following page. If the figures given in Table 25 have significance, it may be said that there was a tendency for robbery and related offenses, stealing, and assault, to be less among this particular group of delinquents than in Manhattan as a whole and in the entire city. Ungovernable behavior, desertion of home, and petty offenses appeared to be greater. The offense of truancy was of less frequent occurrence than in Manhattan as a whole, but of about the same occurrence as for all of the boroughs.

In the absence of specific information showing the nature and extent of the behavior problem existing among the Puerto Rican

[10] The Manhattan health areas are shown by Figure 4. In Figure 3, Brooklyn area 10 lies directly west of the Navy Yard. Brooklyn area 40 contains census tracts 47, 49, 51, 63, and 67, and lies in the center of the area of Figure 3, on the water-front side (p. 105).

group in New York, any opinion about delinquency among them must be based largely upon data of a nonstatistical character. Such an opinion, although appearing to rest upon an agreement among those in close contact with the group, must necessarily be interpreted with caution. As concerning all unskilled groups of workers in New York, the criticism that some of its members are

Table 25. ANALYSIS OF OFFENSES OF 493 DELINQUENT CHILDREN IN SIX HEALTH AREAS WITH A LARGE PUERTO RICAN POPULATION[a]

Offense	Percent of Total			Number		
	Selected Areas	All Manhattan	All Boroughs	Selected Areas	All Manhattan	All Boroughs
Robbery, burglary, and unlawful entry	6.7	8.2	10.9	33	309	1,130
Ungovernable behavior and desertion of home	36.9	31.8	27.1	182	1,196	2,811
Disorderly conduct, peddling, begging, violation of railroad law, violation of corporation ordinance, and unclassified	35.9	33.7	34.9	177	1,269	3,620
Stealing	15.0	18.9	19.5	74	710	2,020
Assault	.8	1.5	2.3	4	56	238
Truancy	4.5	5.4	4.6	22	205	475
Not reported	.2	.5	.7	1	19	80
Total	100.0	100.0	100.0	493	3,764	10,374

Source: Robison, *op. cit.*, Tables 59 and 60.

[a] As previously stated, these health areas are 19, 20, 24, and 25 in Manhattan, and 10 and 40 in Brooklyn. The order of arrangement is the same as given by the author in this source. "Ungovernable behavior" was described as a complex term "applied sometimes to truancy, to manifestations of violent temper, to stealing, to sex offenses, to desertion of home, and to other fields of conflict between parents, or parent surrogates, and children," pp. 124-25.

improvident, gamble, are disinclined to exert themselves although living in poverty, and display signs of antisocial behavior is also prevalent concerning the group of Puerto Ricans living in the Harlem and Brooklyn areas.

These individual reports about the delinquency problem among the Puerto Rican group or the neighborhoods where they live, while of varying significance and reliability, do present interesting points of view. Due to the very nature of their work, reports of law-enforcement officers are probably always biased. Law-abiding Puerto Ricans deeply resent the term "spick," sometimes applied to them by the police, and their reference to Harlem as a "hard" neighborhood. There is also a feeling among the poorest Puerto Ricans in Harlem that the police "have it in for them." The following statement is typical of those obtained from police officers in the Harlem section:

> The areas where the spicks [meaning all Spanish-speaking people] live are the worst in the section. There is no doubt but that most of this neighborhood is unsafe at night. I would not walk down any of these streets at night unless I were armed. The police here usually go in pairs. Often the visitor gets "mugged." By this we mean that a person will jump on you from behind and strike you over the head.

Puerto Ricans themselves say that serious social problems exist among a certain proportion of the group living in these neighborhoods. Contrast the above report with the following statement made by a young, educated Puerto Rican girl who is employed by a large institution in Harlem: "My people go wild when they come to New York. They are not Puerto Ricans anymore. Conditions are so bad in this section that no decent girl of the upper class would walk on these streets at night." The attitude of one of the Puerto Ricans who operated a small grocery store in the East Harlem community is shown by his statements:[11]

> We have been here eight years. I don't know many people. I have three girls. I must protect them. People here in this district do not work. They are not good people. All they do is what you see them doing—nothing. They gamble. I do not bother them. I sell to them only. Business is not good anymore. Too many barber shops; too many pool shops; too many grocery stores. I sit here and sleep—no work.

Such interviews as those given above, although reflecting personal experiences or attitudes of single individuals, tend in every way to bear out the facts shown by the statistics of crime and delinquency for these neighborhoods.

In all immigrant groups which have recently moved to this country, the influences of the mores of the mother country are

[11] Taken from W. E. Hill, "Porto Rican Colonies in New York."

strong. It has been found that the foreign-born, while having higher crime rates than in the mother country, do not have unusually high rates of crime during their early years of residence in this country, and that any problem of this nature arising out of the immigration comes with the second generation, in the difficult period of assimilation and adjustment. In 1930, the last year for which crime statistics can be related to population, practically all of the Puerto Ricans had been in this country for only a few years and many of them had just arrived. There has not been sufficient time for Puerto Rican children to grow up in this country under the social influences found in the Harlem and Brooklyn settlements. The influence of conditions found on the island is, therefore, probably still a strong force affecting behavior in these settlements.

There are important differences in the problem of antisocial behavior on the island and in the United States. The number of homicides according to population is much higher on the island than in the United States. For example, in 1935 the homicide rate for Puerto Rico was 18.2 per 100,000 as compared with about 6 for New York City, and 9 for the entire United States.[12] The common saying in Puerto Rico that most of the crimes of a serious nature are "crimes of passion" arising out of personal difficulties is, perhaps, generally true; also the advice laughingly given to the newcomer about staying out of difficulties by avoiding entanglements of love or politics is not without foundation. Although conditions in Puerto Rico and in the United States are, of course, not comparable, the Puerto Ricans may be right in saying that there is much less organized or planned crime on the island than in many parts of the United States. There are, as would be expected, a considerable number of petty offenses among the poverty-striken mass of people living in the larger island cities. Election frauds have also been the basis of criticism on the island and in Washington, and Puerto Rico has recently enacted a law requiring all voters to appear at the voting place at a particular time and to cast their ballots simultaneously.

There is, at this time, no clear evidence to show what part of

[12] Commissioner of Health of Puerto Rico, *Annual Report*, p. 79.

the antisocial behavior in the communities of settlement here is to be attributed directly to the migration of the Puerto Rican. There may be, as claimed by some, a relation between the high rate of felonies, such as homicide, in Lower Harlem and the character of crime found in Puerto Rico and other countries of the West Indies. The statistics of crime and delinquency of the communities where the Puerto Ricans settle are evidence that as a whole these people are failing to win any degree of financial security and as a result show clear signs of antisocial behavior.

The Puerto Rican migration is an example of an almost peasant people settling in what are probably the most unfavorable urban communities that could be found for them. Although responsibility for creating these conditions cannot be placed on any one cultural group we do know that these distressed people are exposed to unfavorable conditions already existing and possibly made worse by their coming. If this social environment to which the migrant is exposed is considered, together with all of the evidence of other phases of the lack of a successful adjustment in this country, the constantly increasing problem of antisocial behavior in the Puerto Rican settlements cannot but raise a question as to the desirability of a further large migration from the island to these congested areas.[13]

DISINTEGRATING INFLUENCES AFFECTING THE FAMILY

Since many of the families, before coming to this country, have lived under wretched conditions, the movement is usually undertaken under strained circumstances. These facts, together with the worker's low economic status in Harlem, suggest the importance of the disintegrating forces which would affect the family.

Since a majority of the migrants have been in this country for only a few years, the customs and attitudes of the island, as they affect family relations, are still one of the most important influences. As would be expected, these customs and attitudes differ widely from those in the United States. Americans observe in the

---

[13] Alvarado Hernandez, president of the Puerto Rican Spanish League, stated in an interview in 1929 that he estimated that 400,000 people in Puerto Rico were planning or hoping to come to the United States. See William E. Hill, *op. cit.*

Puerto Rican family certain loyalties and affections which seem admirable. Puerto Rican parents display a strong affection for their children. The average Puerto Rican is kind and hospitable to a needy relative, or to a homeless child. Such questions as legitimacy or color are much less important in social and family relations than in the United States. Puerto Ricans follow the customs of other Spanish-speaking countries; the morals of girls and women of the upper class are closely watched. Many Puerto Ricans doubt that the freedom enjoyed by American women would be suitable for their people.

Some of Puerto Rico's most serious social problems, however, are those affecting the family. The protection given to the woman or girl of the higher economic class does not exist for women of the lower-income group. Social problems of illegitimacy, desertion, and consensual relations are common in Puerto Rico. For example, in the decade 1920-30 in Puerto Rico, it was estimated that "those consensually married are about a third as numerous as those married with the established rites."[14] Such relations often give rise to problems of desertion and homeless children.

A considerable number of families among the Harlem and Brooklyn groups show evidence of disintegration due to the migration. At almost all times during the period of migration, it has been easier for women from the island to secure work in New York than for men. For this reason, husbands, in many cases, have remained temporarily on the island. On account of poverty, not all of the other members of the family may be able to move at one time. In the report of one large agency which studied this migration, it was stated that around sixty percent of the families coming to this country from Puerto Rico had left the father behind. Another large agency dealing with a very large number of Puerto Rican families found, by actual tabulation, that the wife of the Puerto Rican family in the Harlem district was almost invariably older than the husband. This was reported as a fact which had been observed for several years. Since this tendency for the wife to be

---

[14] R. C. Foerster, "Racial Problems Involved in Immigration from Latin America and the West Indies to the U.S.," *Bulletin*, U. S. Department of Labor, 1925, p. 38. The statistics showing this fact may be found in many other sources about social conditions in Puerto Rico.

older than the husband does not exist on the island, the implication of such figures is that these marriages, as well as some reported cases of "living together," have taken place in New York, and that there has been a tendency for the female migrant to be older than the male. There is no evidence to show whether the problem of broken marriages or consensual relations exists to any greater degree among the Harlem group of Puerto Ricans than among other groups living under similar conditions. It is a problem often encountered by social workers dealing with this type of family.[15]

Cases of desertion are also rather common. The report of one agency, which was made several years ago, in commenting upon this problem stated that in the Navy Yard section of Brooklyn one-fourth of all of the Puerto Rican families presented problems of domestic relations which often led to desertion and nonsupport.

Other problems affecting the family arise out of poverty. The attempt to pay high rents by doubling up and taking in lodgers has had its social consequences among the poorer families. Since many of the mothers do some sort of sewing or handwork in factories, the problem of the "working mother" also exists. Several years ago when it was comparatively easy for the mother to obtain this light factory work, children were often left with relatives or boarders.

Harlem does not afford a favorable environment for the uneducated and inexperienced girl who comes to New York alone. A girl of this type usually speaks little English, knows nothing about the city, and has had little, or poor, training. In some cases, she finds it necessary to live in a boardinghouse were there are roomers of both sexes. She may also become involved in a highly mixed family situation. Even if this type of girl finds work, it is usually some kind of sewing, or work in making hats, the wages of which

[15] In the study of 25 families in the Navy Yard section of Brooklyn in 1931, 15 were legally married; 4 were "living together" (not common law relations as either the husband or the wife had a living spouse); 2, common law; 3, doubtful, with one party who had previously been married and the death or divorce not verified; and one widower. The Puerto Rican families living in this section are very poor and many are colored. Such a sample should by no means be taken as representative of either the Harlem or the Brooklyn settlement. See Dorothy R. Grotz, "Porto Rican Families in the Navy Yard District of Brooklyn" (typewritten manuscript), Brooklyn Bureau of Charities, 1931.

provide only a bare subsistence. On account of the seriousness of the problem, several years ago one large social organization met the boats coming from Puerto Rico, and endeavored to visit the girls in their homes on the day following arrival. This organization states that it was often difficult or impossible to locate many Spanish-speaking girls who came to the Harlem settlement.

In conclusion, there is sufficient evidence to show that problems of family disintegration exist among the low-income group, and that these problems arise in part from the migration itself and in part from the poor conditions under which many of these individuals and families have to live after they have moved to this country.

THE NEED FOR VOCATIONAL TRAINING

The Puerto Rican migrant's success here is dependent, to a large degree, upon how well and how quickly he can meet the two requirements of language and industrial training. As a whole, the group has not found a successful approach to its problem of language difference and its handicap in the labor market. Up to this time, there has been no organized movement of any importance in New York to meet these needs on the part of the worker. At least, there has been no organization created specifically for this purpose. The worker from the island has been left, much as he saw fit, and without special direction, to take advantage of a course in English at the public library or the Y.M.C.A., or to attend public night school. It appears that the average worker depends upon his work, newspapers, and his associations rather than upon a regular course of instruction to acquire a working knowledge of English. Puerto Ricans, except for the student group in colleges, cling strongly to their own language. Many of them give as the main reason for this the pride in their own language and customs which they profess to have to such a marked degree. Their indifference toward the learning of English is probably to be explained by earlier association with the language on the island.[16] Many Puerto

[16] In seeking an explanation for the indifference of the Puerto Rican toward learning English, the author has most often received the reply that they "just do not like English," or that they "do not like the sound of the language." In Puerto Rico, there

Ricans, even though they may feel friendly toward Americans, believe that their country has been neglected, if not actually mistreated. They have resented the attempt on the part of the United States to teach them English as an encroachment upon their own language and culture. English in their minds is associated with the coming of the sugar interests which bought their lands, and with a culture which many of them do not understand.

It is doubtful that the need for industrial training and general education is being met in a satisfactory manner. Several years ago, a large charity organization visited 120 Spanish-speaking families, selected at random, and inquired about their educational training. As a result of this rather small sample, it was concluded that the majority of the Puerto Rican workers had only a grammar-school education, and that only about five percent of them had gone further than the seventh grade. In 1931, a social worker made a special study of twenty-five families in the Navy Yard district of Brooklyn.[17] Out of forty-nine individuals, it was found in this survey that eighteen were never in school and were illiterate, twenty-four had gone to the fifth grade, four to the seventh grade, and three had been in the first or second year of high school. A social worker with another organization reported that she had made a special effort to get at least one adult in each of sixty Puerto Rican families to attend WPA schools, but that practically all of them were unwilling to attend.

Some observers are of the opinion that the Puerto Rican, as well as members of the other Spanish-speaking groups, is less inclined to seek out educational advantages and follow them up by regular attendance than individuals of some of the other cultural groups. The fact that the Puerto Rican often has to take the first position which is offered to him and work long hours in some unskilled trade could easily account for this apparent lack of interest. His lack of economic security might cause him to be irregular in attendance,

---

is not only an indifference to the learning of English, but, in many cases, an antipathy for it. The recent plan to send American teachers to the island to teach English was resented by many Puerto Ricans.

[17] Grotz, *ibid*. This sample has little significance on account of the few individuals studied. Families in this district are as a rule extremely poor and many of them are colored.

or to drop work which he had undertaken. His inability to understand English and his lack of previous training would prevent him from getting the full value from many of the courses given. Outside of a few organized courses in sewing and domestic work given by social agencies, and instruction in diet given to Puerto Rican mothers, little has been done to provide instruction suitable for the worker of the low-income group.

Not only does the low economic status of the worker affect his ability to overcome rapidly his lack of skill and training, but the poverty of the family appears to have a definite relation to the success of the worker's children in the public schools.[18] Although Puerto Ricans, as a rule profess to be Catholics, they do not send their children to parochial schools. Many Puerto Rican children who enter the public schools in New York speak or understand little English. The children who are transferred from schools in Puerto Rico to those in New York are usually put back in their classes so that they are with children who are two or three years younger than they are. Americans who are teaching Puerto Rican children express the opinion that these children have had less training in discipline and in group coöperation than American children. Lacking the timidity of many of the children in this country, they sometimes act in an unrestrained and impulsive manner. One large agency in the settlement, which has dealt with Puerto Rican children for many years, reported that under proper conditions Puerto Rican children are responsive, easily managed, and affectionate. In contrast to this, another large institution said that for some reason which they could not explain, the Puerto Rican children were more destructive than any group of children with whom they had had contact. All the evidence obtainable shows the relation of unsatisfactory home conditions to difficulties at school. During the past few years the desperate economic condition of these families has caused them to move so frequently that it has often been difficult to locate the children when they did not attend school.

[18] The reader interested in mental ability tests should see C. P. Armstrong and associates, *Reaction of Puerto Rican Children in New York City to Psychological Tests*. It is not the purpose of this study to raise the question of the innate ability of the migrant.

Social Adjustment

RECREATIONAL AND SOCIAL OUTLETS

Certain social barriers found on the island continue to exist for the Harlem group in New York. In Puerto Rico, the worker of the low-income group lives under what may be called a sort of economic class system. People of the "second class" do not, under any condition, attend "first class" social functions. The social status of an individual is known and accepted by him and by all the people of his community. This attitude continues to exist in New York, and affects social relations between the educated and successful Spanish-speaking individual, and the people living in Harlem. Many Spanish-speaking people in New York refuse to identify themselves with the Harlem group in any way. The upper-class Latin American, whether he be from Puerto Rico, Colombia, or any of the other countries, refers to the Harlem settlement as one of "working people." The Puerto Rican of the upper class attempts to explain unfavorable conditions in Lower Harlem by the fact that so many people of the very poorest class have migrated to this country from the island. Only a few prominent Puerto Ricans, who almost invariably live outside of the settlement, have ever attempted to provide it with any sort of leadership or to assist in the solution of the problems of the people.

Language difficulty, poverty, and the concentration and isolation of the settlement cause the social activities of the Puerto Rican worker to be largely within his own group. Many of the migrants of the low-income group, having only a limited knowledge of the city and not speaking English, are hesitant about venturing outside of the particular area which they have come to know. The fact that they settle in a particular neighborhood and are able to continue the customs and social activities of the island greatly lessens their problem of social adjustment in the new community. The activities on the island continue to be the main ones among the group here. The men still converse on island politics, and the young people still attend dances, especially on Saturday nights. Many of the Puerto Rican dances are sponsored by social organizations, and there are a number of halls suitable for this purpose in the neighborhood. Argentine or Mexican films are often shown in the moving picture houses, which are patronized by large numbers of Spanish-speaking people. Music, in Harlem as on the island, holds an important place, and guitars are found in many of the homes. American-made guitars have almost crowded the four-stringed "cuatro," which is sometimes used in Puerto Rico, out of existence; and the beautiful nightly serenades of Puerto Rico seem also to have been abandoned in New York.

The activities of the children, because of school and play, are of course, less confined to their own group. Puerto Rican children and young people take part in various forms of entertainment, such as plays, Christmas exercises, and study clubs, provided for them by organizations such as the Union Settlement. The Heckscher Foundation for children is another large organization which provides organized play for the children of the neighborhood. The play life of a majority of the children, however, is still an individual matter, and is on the street. Children mingle with those of other racial groups, and quickly begin to feel the influence of American customs.

Puerto Ricans in the Harlem section have many social organizations, and new ones are constantly being formed. The purpose of an organization may vary from the independence of Puerto Rico to a social outlet for a small group of people from Ponce or some other city on the island. If a group of people from one town in Puerto Rico form a club, this does not mean that they will not take in members from other towns. Some of the members of these social clubs are particularly active at election time, which would seem to indicate that they have political sponsorship. The head of a large recreational institution in the neighborhood reported that she had found considerable difficulty in organizing a large number of Puerto Ricans in a single group on account of petty dissension caused by so many small organizations. Few of the smaller groups or clubs appear to be permanent, and many of them are constantly being broken up to be again formed into new associations.

American influence is largely responsible for the Puerto Ricans' pronounced interest in prize fighting. Many young Puerto Ricans enter this sport and some of them have become successful fighters. Among their well-known fighters, most of whom are in the lightweight class, is one champion of the bantam-weight class who is practically the idol of the group in New York. There are usually several Puerto Rican contestants in the Dykeman Oval in a single evening, and these contests draw a large and enthusiastic support from the Harlem section. Pictures of Puerto Rican fighters are frequently seen on the walls of bars and grills in the settlement.

The fact that the Puerto Ricans live in mixed and congested communities not only affects relations in the matters of employment and housing, as has previously been pointed out, but has an important effect on social relations. Some of the conflicts already referred to result from the differences between the Latin-American groups themselves, the apparent dislike for the person of Oriental blood, and the attitude of the Puerto Rican toward the American-born Negro. One study reported that the Brazilians in the Navy Yard section of Brooklyn have a deep dislike for the Puerto Ricans.[19] This conflict is largely the result of language and racial differences. As a rule, however, where both of the cultural groups speak Spanish, these differences are nothing more than provincial and petty quarrels. Several explanations might be found for the apparent dislike of the Puerto Rican for the Oriental. It has been suggested that a probable cause of this attitude among the West Indian groups is the fact that the Chinese have been imported as laborers into some of the Latin-American countries where they occupy an inferior position.[20] In the entire island of Puerto Rico, however, there are only a few persons of Oriental blood. If this is an explanation of the feeling of the Puerto Ricans, it would have to result from the influence of other Latin-American groups rather than from direct association with Chinese or other Orientals in Puerto Rico. Insofar as the Puerto Rican is concerned, it seems far more probable that such an attitude comes about in this country because of economic conflicts in certain lines of work such as that connected with hotels and restaurants; and also, as in the case of

[19] Crime Commission of New York State, *A Study of Delinquency in a District of King's County*, p. 9.

[20] The writer is indebted to Ira de A. Reid, Professor of Sociology at Atlanta University and a student of racial relations in Harlem for many years, for his help in checking some of the information obtained from interviews on social relations in Harlem. The reader should see his forthcoming study on the subject of Negro migration to the United States.

the Mexican in California, because of resentment of the attentions paid by young Filipinos to Spanish-speaking women.

Far more important than these differences between Latin-American groups or their relations with the Oriental is the complex problem which grows out of the matter of color. As has already been said, although the attitude varies with the economic class, in Puerto Rico there is much less general discrimination on the basis of color than here. Because Puerto Ricans living in the Harlem section are often a mixture of several cultural elements, the presence of some degree of Negro blood does not cause an individual to be treated as though he belongs to a distinct social class, as it would in some parts of the United States. Toward Puerto Ricans who are entirely Negro, however, the attitude of the group is less favorable.

Although it is true that among the low-income group of Puerto Ricans in Harlem language is far more important in forming social relations than the presence of Negro blood, the attitude of the Puerto Rican toward the American Negro, a person outside the group, is radically different. Finding the American-born Negro confronted with serious disadvantages in this country, the Puerto Ricans want to maintain their own group and to distinguish themselves from him because they believe that through this means they will avoid his social position. People who have studied the social relations of the West Indian groups in Harlem report that there appears to be an interesting correlation between the color of the West Indian and his desire to be distinguished from the American Negro. It seems that the darker the person from the West Indies is, the more intense is his desire to speak only Spanish, and to do so in a louder voice.[21] Puerto Ricans avoid moving into houses which are inhabited entirely by American Negro families. They will not send their children to summer camps with the Negro children. Since it is difficult for the social agencies of Harlem to provide separate camps, this means that many Puerto Rican children do not attend. Probably the outstanding fact about the racial attitude of the Puerto Rican in Harlem is that he insists upon being distinguished

---

[21] This interesting information was called to the writer's attention by Professor Reid.

from the American Negro. This attitude may well be shown by the remark made when a young American woman told a Puerto Rican boy who worked in a drug store near her home that her sister had gone to visit in Puerto Rico. "Well," he said, "That is good. When she returns, she can tell the people here that we are not all Negroes." Many other examples could be given which would bring out this attitude. On the other hand, the American Negro does not appear to be particularly anxious to fraternize with the Puerto Rican. This is often shown by his criticism of the Puerto Rican's manner of living. Since the Puerto Rican speaks Spanish, he is the object of some of the feeling, already mentioned, which the Negro born in this country has for all of the people who migrate from the West Indies.

Within the group, the attitude of the Puerto Rican with regard to color seems to be affected by the length of residence in this country. It is the opinion of those who have studied the group for many years that the white Puerto Rican, after he has lived in New York for several years, takes up what is described as the "American attitude" on the question of color. This change greatly affects his relations with all Spanish-speaking people who have any noticeable degree of Negro blood and intensifies his feeling against the American Negro. This feeling, if developed generally among the group, would in time cause the Puerto Rican Negro to be neglected by his own people and those of other groups. It would be another ground for resentment against the "color line" found here on the part of the colored person who comes to this country from Puerto Rico.

THE MIGRANT'S REACTION TO RELIGIOUS AND POLITICAL INFLUENCES

The average Puerto Rican worker who moves to New York usually does not seek or rely upon the influence and aid of the church in making his economic and social adjustments in his new home. Puerto Ricans are usually Catholic in religion, but many of them have no formal affiliation with the Church in New York. Every source of information, without exception, and representing both Catholic and Protestant points of view, stresses the lack of contact with the Church on the part of a large number of the group. Catholic workers find among them a greater need for religious instruction than among other Spanish-speaking groups. They have found that many couples nominally Catholic have been married only by a civil ceremony, and it is not uncommon to discover among them a child of five or six years of age who has not been baptized. The lack of devotion to the rules of the Church, as might be expected, is much more pronounced among the men than among the women.

Although the same religious conditions as described above are found in Puerto Rico, some of the group here feel that the migration has caused a further drifting away from the Church. One Puerto Rican social worker who has lived in the Harlem section for many years and is in almost daily contact with about fifty or sixty Puerto Rican families believes that this lack of contact with the Church in New York is due to the work of Protestant and nonsectarian organizations among them. Another person thoroughly familiar with the Puerto Rican in Harlem points to their almost universal sympathy for the Loyalist cause in Spain as evidence of a lack of the influence of the Church, and attributes the reason for this to a natural outgrowth of the wretched condition of the masses in Puerto Rico. Another Puerto Rican social worker finds the cause for the lack of religious influence in the many attractions of the large city which divert the Puerto Rican from religious service and an interest in Church affairs. A Puerto Rican student reported that among the younger people there was a feeling that their people had been neglected by the Church as well as by other organizations. Many others recognize the lack of a close association with the Church, but are unable to assign any one particular reason for it.

Outside of the Catholic Church, the Pentecostal and other similar faiths have attracted many of the Puerto Ricans. The groups often meet in the homes and hold prayer meetings, and there are small churches in the Harlem community. Several churches of the more common Protestant faiths have always existed in New York for the Spanish-speaking people.

Although a few Protestant religious societies have been interested particularly in the Puerto Ricans, the institution of greatest

Social Adjustment

influence among them in New York is not the church but the nonsectarian charity organization. In Puerto Rico, vast sums have been spent by these organizations to feed people who were practically starving, and they have played a large part during all years of the migration in relieving distressed families here. These organizations, however, are likely to be considered Protestant by the Puerto Rican.

Some of the political influences affecting the migrant in Harlem are indicated by the parades and demonstrations which in recent years have come to be almost a part of the life in the colony. Saturday afternoons and Sundays are favorite days for these events, and numbers of Puerto Ricans usually take part in them. The demonstrations are sometimes in connection with independence for the island, a question which, as might be expected, is of great interest to them. Nationalist campaigns for independence in Puerto Rico have extended to the settlement in New York, and organizations for independence have been formed and small contributions are sent back to the island for the cause. During the recent trouble growing out of the independence movement on the island, the sympathy of the group in New York was apparently entirely on the side of those favoring independence. The parade which took place some time after the indictment of Albizu-Campos by Federal authorities was a typical Harlem demonstration of first rank:[22]

> Ten thousand Puerto Ricans, representing a score of political and social clubs, paraded for three hours through the streets of Lower Harlem yesterday afternoon to protest the attitude and actions of "Imperialistic America" in making slaves of the natives of the island. Spurred on by Representative Vito Marcantonio, who recently returned from a two-weeks visit to the island and denounced conditions there, the paraders shouted "Free Puerto Rico" and "Down with Yankee Imperialism" so loudly that thousands of other residents in the area, populated mostly by Negroes and Spaniards, leaned out of the windows and over the edges of roof tops and added their protests to those of the demonstrators.

Intense excitement prevails at all of these demonstrations; there are numerous banners, people are protesting, and women are talking in high-pitched voices.

[22] New York *Times,* August 30, 1936.

Although a majority of the Puerto Ricans are professed Catholics, they are, as has already been brought out, almost invariably in sympathy with the Loyalists in Spain. If there are any Fascist sympathizers, they are not in evidence at the demonstrations over this issue. When the Spanish Rebels bombarded Madrid in the summer of 1936, the Puerto Rican group took an active part in the parade of protest in which several thousand children in the Harlem section marched. This parade was arranged by churches, schools, and trade unions as a protest against Fascism and war, and was one of numerous demonstrations which have taken place. Placards of "Down with Fascist Aid," "La Contra Revolution Fascista Española," and "Viva el Frente Popular Español" were in evidence. As in the case of the worker's attitude toward strikes, so might this sympathy for the Loyalist cause be partly accounted for by the fact that many of the Puerto Ricans are Socialists.

In addition to the influences found in Harlem, the migrant often shows the influence of the disturbed political status of Puerto Rico. He has associated the suffering and poverty of his people with the colonial status of the island, the holding of land by the large corporations, and what he considers the failure of the United States to treat the Puerto Rican people with whole-hearted equality. Puerto Ricans in New York often complain that their lands have been taken from them, and refer bitterly to the causes which they say made them leave their native island.[23] Puerto Ricans for many years have heard the complaints of their Latin-American neighbors against "Yankee imperialism." On account of such influences, which start with childhood, the Puerto Rican often blames social organization for the ills of his people. The unfortunate Puerto

[23] Americans, in turn, point to a comparison of the conditions of health, sanitation, and education on the island in 1898 and at the present time. There was hardly a school building in Puerto Rico at the time of the American occupation. Health conditions were deplorable at that time. The actual amount of the investment in the sugar industry of Puerto Rico is not large (thirty million dollars); it is much less even than the appropriation for public works given to Puerto Rico by the last Administration (forty million dollars). Puerto Rico does not pay taxes to the Federal government, and taxes collected in the United States on its tobacco are refunded to the island. The same is true for the tariff on articles imported by Puerto Ricans. Although the concentration of land in large farms may complicate Puerto Rico's situation, the fundamental economic problem is the meager resources available for the large population.

Rican on relief usually becomes a member of the Workers Alliance. All reports state that he is not behind any of the other racial groups in his willingness to join a demonstration at the Home Relief Office. During the last few years there also have been many campaigns by Communist organizations in the Harlem area.

Between the two major political parties, the Puerto Rican is almost without exception Democratic. It was during the adminstration of Wilson that the citizenship measure was passed; in 1928, the Democratic party platform contained a declaration favoring Puerto Rico's admission as a state; and the present administration has done much to relieve suffering on the island by the expenditure of large sums of money.

Politically, the Puerto Ricans are now combined with other groups under a leadership which is not Puerto Rican. These political leaders in the Harlem district have gained influence with the group by declaring their sympathy for the movement for Puerto Rican independence, condemning the treatment of the island by the United States, and constantly pressing for more liberal aid for the distressed people living in the Harlem area.

CHAPTER IX

General Summary and Conclusion

THE MIGRATION of the Puerto Rican to New York is another example of the old and never-ceasing movement of people who hope to better their condition. It constitutes an important part of the well-known and much larger general movement of people to New York and other cities which has been taking place in recent years. The Puerto Rican, finding himself landless, unemployed, and herded with others into his native towns and cities, has for some time begun to look to the United States as a possible means of escape from economic conditions and poverty which almost beggar description. He has, as have the people of other cultural groups, come to New York to earn the high money wages paid in this country and to take the place of European immigrant groups which are now restricted.

Certain important differences exist, however, between the migration of the Puerto Rican and that of some of the other groups. The movement of the Puerto Rican is to particular areas of one large city, rather than one from rural sections to various cities. Due to better steamship facilities between the island and New York as compared with those between the island and the Gulf ports, there are no important places of settlement outside of New York for people from the island. In contrast to the migration from many of the Latin-American countries, that of the Puerto Rican grows largely out of the consequences of population pressure. There is little doubt but that the poverty suffered by the Puerto Rican in his native island is even greater than that of the Negro in the South. Except that required of people from some of the other Latin-American countries, the adjustment due to change in climate, is greater for the Puerto Rican than for other immigrant groups. In contrast to some of the groups, the Puerto Rican is a citizen of this country, he is given free entry, and he is already familiar with many of the institutions found here. This movement has, however, many things in common with the movements of other groups. It is of very recent origin and is based largely upon economic motives, and the migrants are essentially rural people.

When the migration is examined from the standpoint of the migrant, it is impossible to state categorically whether or not the Puerto Rican has materially benefited by moving to the Harlem or Navy Yard sections of New York. Both in this country and in Puerto Rico the economic status of the worker is far below a satisfactory standard. Due to the fact that he is often unemployed and is confronted by an urban environment where there is an increased cost of living which must be met by regular money payments, his position here may be even less secure than it was on a tropical island where the subsistence level is much lower. Although by coming to this country he does escape from what may be thought of as an economic "class system," he finds here what he terms discrimination and prejudice. The Puerto Rican who has Negro blood also finds a color line, which does not exist, at least to the same degree, on the island. The amount of dependency existing at the present time among the group shows that most of them are living on the narrowest fringe of economic security. The Puerto Rican lives under as crowded and unsatisfactory housing conditions as any group in New York. Equally bad are his health conditions. A longer period of residence in this country cannot help but bring out more forcibly the social consequence of such an environment and such conditions upon the migrant.

The social adjustment necessitated by the migration results from the abrupt change of people but slightly removed from the peasant class from a simple rural environment to the slum section of an enormous city. The migration causes disintegrating forces to affect the family. In addition to this painful adjustment, the worker and his family are exposed to conditions which have long been recognized as harmful to the happiness and well-being of all people regardless of background. Often mixed with other families under extremely crowded conditions, without funds or employment, and in many cases suffering from malnutrition or some chronic disease, it is not strange that the worker and his family feel the influence of the antisocial behavior which is prevalent in these neighborhoods. Having come from an island where he has already acquired a feeling of mistreatment at the hands of the American people and their government, he is often resentful as a result of the clash in culture, racial antagonisms, and the failure to realize many expectations because of what he feels are discrimination and indifference.

There is no doubt but that community and philanthropic services in New York are far superior to those of Puerto Rico. Puerto Ricans in New York, along with other cultural groups, receive the benefits of a much wider and more generous social program than that existing in the majority of communities of the United States.

From the standpoint of the community, certain effects of the migration are clear. As a rule the migrant can satisfy only the demand for unskilled work. In addition to this, the Puerto Rican worker is not as familiar with American customs as is the American-born Negro, and does not have the Negro's ability to speak English. He suffers the same language handicap, usually has less skill, faces a greater adjustment on account of climate and differences in environment, and lacks the physical strength of the majority of the European immigrant stocks. Since there is already a pressing demand for slum clearance in Harlem and in other neighborhoods where the Puerto Ricans have a tendency to concentrate, the migration of a very large number of people from the crowded districts of the island could easily complicate still further the housing and neighborhood situations already existing in these areas. In some respects, the migration of the Puerto Rican has had the same effect upon the community health conditions as that of the Negro. The apparent susceptibility of the Puerto Rican to tuberculosis and the incidence of this disease among them is much greater than that found among the American-born colored groups. Parasitical diseases present a special health problem arising out of the migration. As with the influx of Southern Negroes, there are other problems of crime, education, race contacts, and even some with political aspects. Because of the difference in culture and the environment which has conditioned the migrant before his arrival in this country, practically the same problem of assimilation exists for the Puerto Rican as for the non-citizen immigrant groups. To the extent that the Puerto Rican feels that the American occupation of his native island has resulted in an encroachment upon his own culture, and to the extent that he therefore retains the attitudes which result from and go with an aroused nationalism among his people, this problem of assimilation will be made more difficult.

Whether or not these conditions will obtain in future years will depend mainly upon what improvement can be made in the economic status of the Puerto Rican people on the island. The prospects of rapidly improving these present standards are not encouraging. On the other hand, as population pressure grows more unbearable, migration to New York, and this in large numbers, will result.

A beginning study of this nature cannot help but suggest many other topics connected with the Puerto Rican migrant in New York which are worthy of investigation. A study of the migration by the case method, as suggested in the introductory chapter, by tracing and developing information about particular families and individuals who have moved from the island to New York, would fill many important gaps in the information about the group. The work of the social agency among the group is so important that it could well constitute a separate study. The need for statistical information, already pointed out, also exists, particularly regarding occupations, degree of skill, economic status, and health conditions of the people who are migrating. Without this information, it will always be difficult to answer specific questions about the type of individual who is coming from the island to New York. Other phases of the migration which deserve study and development are employment, the industrial ability of the worker, and the problem of racial contacts. Certain specialists are already planning to publish the results of several years of study on the health problems of the group. At the present time the Puerto Ricans constitute such an important group in Harlem that any of the many general studies of housing, crime, or other social problems in this area can hardly omit them.

Appendices

APPENDIX A

Notes on Method and Materials Used in the Selection of Areas Having a Large Puerto Rican Population

ON ALL phases of the migration, there is a scarcity of published sources. Even recent studies, while devoting considerable space to the Filipino, Hawaiian, and other smaller groups, contain little or no discussion of the Puerto Rican migrant.[1] There is no organization among the Puerto Ricans in New York, similar to the Urban League for the Negroes or similar organizations of other groups, which collects information of a statistical nature about its own people. Due to these facts, the student of the Puerto Rican migration has little published material which he may use as a guide or as a means of checking his own conclusions.

Probably the outstanding difficulty in connection with the selection of an area of settlement is the fact that so little data about the group is given in the Federal census. Puerto Ricans, as has already been pointed out, are classified by the census reports as "native-born." The National Tuberculosis Association has, however, classified the persons born in Puerto Rico and living in New York in 1930 according to statistical areas of the city. The Welfare Council, using these data, has prepared a map showing the number of Puerto Ricans in each statistical area.

Even if data from the census of 1930, according to census tracts, were available, only the location of the group at one particular time would be shown. The population in a community such as Harlem is constantly changing. The Puerto Rican group itself has constantly been expanding and extending its neighborhood of settlement since the first entrance of Puerto Ricans into East Harlem. In spite of these difficulties, there is enough data avail-

[1] For example, Brown and Roucek, *Our Racial and National Minorities*.

able to show a marked tendency for the Puerto Ricans to concentrate in particular areas in the city, and also to define these areas with a fair degree of accuracy.

As was pointed out in Chapter IV (see Table 17, p. 64), 31,722 persons out of a total of 44,908 who were born in Puerto Rico lived in the statistical areas M-8C and M-6C of Manhattan, and K-1 and K-3 of Brooklyn (see p. 63 for the boundaries of these areas). Of the total number, 19,223 Puerto Ricans lived in the statistical area M-8C. The data from the census of 1930 definitely locate the general place of residence of more than seventy percent of the group living in New York in 1930. For the purpose of studying housing conditions, these statistical areas are, however, too large; besides, they contain certain districts in which few Puerto Ricans live.

Another source of reliable information about the settlement of the group is to be found in the quarterly bulletin of 1934 of the Department of Health of New York City:[2]

> In Manhattan the Porto Ricans are found chiefly in the district which adjoins the northern portion of Central Park, the southern boundary being on the east side about 93rd Street, and the northern boundary about 130th Street. In Brooklyn the Porto Ricans are most numerous along the waterfront from the Navy Yard south to Gowanus Canal and extending inland to about Third Avenue.

This location of their settlements conforms to that of the statistical areas of the census, but is more restricted. No eastern or western boundaries are given for the Harlem settlement.

Another source of published data is the map showing the racial groups of Harlem, reproduced on page 95. Its value lies in the fact that it indicates the character of the population by blocks. Unfortunately for our purposes, this study does not include the East Harlem section. Except for East Harlem, this map makes possible a fairly accurate location of the Spanish-speaking groups and also shows the areas of greatest concentration.

The areas of the concentration of Puerto Rican people are shown by Sophia M. Robison in her study of delinquent children.[3]

[2] Vol. II, 1934, No. 4, p. 79.
[3] *Can Delinquency Be Measured?*

Dr. Robison classified the number of children referred as delinquents in the year 1930 by cultural groups according to health areas. It was found in this study that 92 out of a total of 144 Puerto Rican children referred to agencies as delinquent in 1930 lived in health areas 19, 20, 24, and 25 of Manhattan, and areas 10 and 40 of Brooklyn (see p. 137). The largest numbers, 22 and 26, came from Manhattan health areas 19 and 20.

Using all of the data above, derived from published sources, the areas of settlement were tentatively marked out. Then the tentative selections were submitted to social agencies that were doing work in these particular neighborhoods for suggestions and corrections. Where there was a case of doubt as to the boundary to be selected for a certain area, the area was inspected and an attempt was made to use any facts obtained in this manner. In the Harlem section, it was decided to bound the area on the west by Eighth Avenue and on the east by Third Avenue. It was also thought best to begin the settlement at 98th Street and end it at 126th Street (see boundaries, p. 93). The Brooklyn area follows almost exactly the area of settlement defined by the Department of Health given in the quotation above.

Only approximately three-fourths of the Puerto Ricans in New York live in the areas selected, and it is not claimed that the streets selected as boundaries mark the exact places where the settlements begin. Where only a small area was involved, some consideration has been given to the boundaries of health areas and other statistical units. A large area has been selected, rather than census tracts where there was the greatest concentration of Puerto Rican people. A few of the census tracts are largely Negro, but numerous Puerto Ricans do live in them. The same is true with regard to one tract in the East Harlem section, where there is a dense concentration of Italian people. There are, of course, many Puerto Ricans living west of Eighth Avenue along Manhattan Avenue, and there are also Puerto Ricans east of and on Second Avenue. Instead of attempting to mark the settlement by numerous small and irregular boundaries, an attempt is made only to define an area which will give the housing conditions of a majority of the group, and afford a comparison of the general housing conditions found with those of other sections. Due to the fact that a large area was purposely selected, the data presented probably shows more favorable conditions than would have been shown if the census tracts of the greatest concentration of Puerto Rican people had been selected.

Appendix B

Data on Residential and Dwelling Units for Selected Areas in New York City

	Percent of Total Classified					Number				
	Selected Area Harlem	Selected Area Brooklyn	Total Manhattan	Lower East Side Health District	Central Harlem Health District	Selected Area Harlem	Selected Area Brooklyn	Total Manhattan	Lower East Side Health District	Central Harlem Health District
	(1)	(2)	(3)	(4)	(5)	(1)	(2)	(3)	(4)	(5)
Structures										
Age										
Less than 10 years	1.56	2.25	4.06	4.22	1.75	72	316	2,290	429	113
10 years and under 20	1.10	1.25	3.91	1.49	1.38	51	174	2,212	152	89
20 years and under 35	7.91	2.07	10.99	5.62	9.99	366	290	6,209	571	644
35 years and older	89.43	94.43	81.04	88.67	86.88	4,136	13,227	45,787	9,019	5,600
Condition										
Good condition	12.60	16.71	24.92	12.58	14.40	583	2,341	14,077	1,279	928
Needs minor repairs	69.35	58.44	54.85	53.30	65.84	3,207	8,186	30,991	5,421	4,244
Needs major repairs	15.50	16.48	15.93	24.82	17.11	717	2,308	9,000	2,525	1,103
Unfit for use	2.55	8.37	4.30	9.30	2.65	118	1,172	2,430	946	171
Total						4,625	14,007	56,498	10,171	6,446
Family quarters										
Total number						39,247	44,545	590,767	111,394	49,440
Occupied						33,319	36,667	485,623	87,562	42,026
Vacant	15.10	17.69	17.80	21.39	15.00	5,928	7,878	105,144	23,832	7,414

Data on Residential and Dwelling Units for Selected Areas in New York City (*Cont.*)

	Percent of Total Classified					Number				
	Selected Area Harlem	Selected Area Brooklyn	Total Man-hattan	Lower East Side Health District	Central Harlem Health District	Selected Area Harlem	Selected Area Brooklyn	Total Manhattan	Lower East Side Health District	Central Harlem Health District
Number of Families										
1930 Census						32,041	36,833	468,956	83,538	42,098
1934 real property inventory						36,688	37,522	501,099	88,607	47,166
Increase	14.50	1.87	6.85	6.07	12.04	4,647	689	32,143	5,069	5,068
Equipment[a]										
With mechanical refrigeration	9.91	10.09	30.40	7.70	8.68	3,302	3,700	147,603	6,431	3,644
Without tub or shower	7.05	43.15	25.16	50.98	5.07	2,349	15,820	122,194	44,638	2,129
Without private indoor toilet	7.42	37.18	23.65	51.60	4.12	2,472	13,632	114,844	45,184	1,732
Rentals (per rented occupied family quarters)										
Under $10.00	1.98	3.66	3.38	10.31	1.19	651	1,091	16,046	8,944	484
$10.00 to $19.99	13.61	35.01	20.97	47.12	8.44	4,472	10,423	99,378	40,861	3,484
$20.00 to $29.99	39.15	33.16	21.49	22.20	24.55	12,867	9,874	101,834	19,250	10,161
$30.00 to $49.99	34.91	18.73	27.22	13.19	52.12	11,474	5,577	129,008	11,432	21,590
$50.00 to $74.99	7.83	5.21	13.01	3.78	11.91	2,574	1,552	61,637	3,280	4,884
$75.00 to $99.99	1.60	2.41	5.70	1.47	1.60	525	716	27,028	1,276	656
$100.00 to $149.99	.28	1.20	4.33	1.13	.13	92	358	20,547	978	52
$150.00 and over	.64	.62	3.90	.80	.06	209	184	18,509	695	23
Total						32,864	29,775	473,987	86,716	41,334

Rental *per room* (all occupied family quarters in multi-structures only)

Under $3.00	4.05	5.63	3.42	6.75	2.03	1,302	1,345	15,771	5,658	829
$3.00 to $4.99	15.85	36.61	16.11	36.48	8.69	5,092	8,739	74,265	30,579	3,546
$5.00 to $5.99	27.29	18.84	14.82	20.95	16.64	8,765	4,496	68,321	17,567	6,786
$6.00 to $6.99	19.18	10.24	11.12	11.46	16.72	6,161	2,443	51,272	9,611	6,818
$7.00 to $9.99	23.51	11.09	17.70	12.96	37.87	7,553	2,646	81,610	10,866	15,444
$10.00 to $19.99	9.03	8.82	20.57	5.82	16.74	2,899	2,106	94,848	4,879	6,829
$20.00 to $34.99	.61	5.60	10.29	3.11	1.12	197	1,336	47,427	2,604	457
$35.00 and over	.48	3.17	5.97	2.47	.19	156	758	27,515	2,070	78
Total						32,125	23,869	461,029	83,834	40,787

Source: *New York Real Property Inventory, 1934.*
[a] Percentage based on number of occupied family quarters.

Appendix C

Boundaries and Census Tracts in the Settlements Studied

Central Harlem

Boundaries (beginning at northwest corner of the area and giving first the northern boundary, then the eastern, then the southern, and finally the western): Eighth Avenue and Harlem River; Harlem River; Third Avenue; East 119th Street to Fifth Avenue, and West 110th Street to Eighth Avenue; Eighth Avenue.

Census Tracts

186	204	216	228
190	206	218	230
196	208	220	232
198	210	222	234
200	212	224	236
	214	226	

Lower East Side

Boundaries: East 42d Street and Park; East 42d Street to Third Avenue, and East 34th Street to East River; East River; James Slip, and New Chambers; Park Row, Bowery, Fourth Avenue, Park Avenue.

Census Tracts

2	18	34	60
4	20	36	62
6	22	38	64
8	24	40	66
10	26	42	68
12	27	44	70
14	28	46	72
16	30	48	80
	32	50	

Appendices

Brooklyn Settlement

CENSUS TRACTS[1]

1	27	53	75
3	29	55	77
5	31	55.1	79
7	33	57	81
9	35	57.1	83
11	37	59	85
13	39	61	87
15	41	63	89
17	43	65	91
19	45	67	93
21	47	69	95
23	49	71	125
25	51	73	127

[1] See *Real Property Inventory*, Brooklyn Borough, Tables 1 to 4, inclusive.

Bibliography

Bibliography

No attempt is made to give a complete bibliography of the social and economic problems of Puerto Rico. The books listed below will be sufficient to give the reader a good understanding of these problems, and they constitute the important sources of data about the island. Comments have been added when it was believed that they would be helpful. A few studies which are not directly connected with the migration have been listed because they afford valuable bases for comparison or are sources of general information which might be helpful to the reader. The place of reference for unpublished sources has been indicated.

Adams, Romanzo, Interracial Marriage in Hawaii, Macmillan Company, New York, 1937.

> Puerto Ricans now constitute about two percent of the total population of Hawaii. The author points out that the type of Puerto Rican who has migrated to Hawaii, which represents an adverse selection, has not been able to adjust himself to the conditions found there. Although these Puerto Ricans have been in Hawaii for many years, their progress has been unfavorable when compared with that of other groups.

Armstrong, C. P., and Associates, Reactions of Puerto Rican Children in New York City to Psychological Tests, a report of the Special Committee on Immigration and Naturalization, Chamber of Commerce of the State of New York, 1935 (printed pamphlet).

Barceló, Antonio P., In Defense of Porto Rico, Bureau of Supplies, Printing, and Transportation, San Juan, P.R., 1928.

> Mr. Barceló is one of the prominent political leaders of the island. A group in Puerto Rico had sent to President Coolidge a request for a freer form of government. This book is in answer to the reply which was received from President Coolidge to the effect that the United States had never made any promise to Puerto Rico which had not been more than fulfilled.

Bary, Helen V., Child Welfare in the Insular Possessions of the United States, U. S. Department of Labor, Children's Bureau, Publication No. 127, Part I, Porto Rico, 1923.

Bourne, Dorothy D., Puerto Rico's Predicament, Survey, July, 1936.

Bourne, J. R., First Report: see Puerto Rican Emergency Relief Administration.

Brown, F. J., and J. S. Roucek, Our Racial and National Minorities, Prentice-Hall, Inc., 1937.

Carrol, H. K., Report on the Island of Porto Rico, U. S. Government Printing Office, 1899.

> This report is that of a special commissioner sent by President McKinley to investigate conditions on the island. An extremely valuable study for the purpose of comparing conditions at the time of the American occupation with those of today.

Catholic Charities of the Archdiocese of New York, Survey of Spanish Population in the Archdiocese of New York (typewritten manuscript, 91 pp., on file in office of Catholic Charities).

Cebollero, Pedro A., Reactions of Puerto Rican Children in New York City to Psychological Tests, San Juan, P.R., 1936 (printed pamphlet). A criticism of the tests given by Dr. Armstrong. See above.

Chaddock, Robert E., Principles and Methods of Statistics, Houghton Mifflin Company, New York, 1925.

Clark, Victor S., and Associates, Porto Rico and Its Problems, Brookings Institution, Washington, 1930.

> This book represents the combined work of several scholars in their fields of specialization. It is perhaps the most valuable study which has been made on Puerto Rico.

Committee on Mineral Resources of Puerto Rico, Report, Bureau of Supplies, Printing, and Transportation, San Juan, P.R., 1934.

DeGolia, D., Tariff Problems of Puerto Rico: see Puerto Rican Emergency Relief Administration.

Diffie, B. W. and J. W., Porto Rico: a Broken Pledge, Vanguard Press, Inc., New York, 1931.

> A study in American imperialism as it applies to Puerto Rico. Raises the question as as to whether the condition of the Puerto Rican has improved during the period of the American occupation. Shows protest of people on the island to what they consider neglect and mistreatment at the hands of the American government.

Domingo, W. A., The Tropics in New York, *Survey*, March 1, 1925.

> This discusses the racial conflicts encountered by the West Indian in New York.

Enamorado-Cuesta, J., Porto Rico—Past and Present, Eureka Printing Company, New York, 1929.

> This gives a good account of the development of the political parties on the island.

Feldman, Herman, Racial Factors in American Industry, Harper & Brothers, New York, 1931.

Fleagle, Fred K., Social Problems in Porto Rico, D. C. Heath & Company, Boston, 1917.

An excellent survey of social conditions by the former chancellor of the University of Puerto Rico. Somewhat out-of-date, but still a valuable study.

Foerster, Robert F., The Racial Problems Involved in Immigration from Latin America and the West Indies to the United States, U. S. Department of Labor, Government Printing Office, 1926.

The thesis of this study is that immigration from these countries represents an adverse selection for the United States on account of the large Negro and Indian elements in their populations.

Ford, James, and Others, Slums and Housing, Harvard University Press, Cambridge, Mass., 1936 (2 vols.).

A coöperative work by many scholars on housing, written with special reference to New York City.

Franklin, Charles L., The Negro Labor Unionist of New York City, Columbia University Press, New York, 1936.

A valuable study of the relation of the Negro worker in New York to the trade union.

Grotz, Dorothy R., Porto Rican Families in the Navy Yard District of Brooklyn, 1931 (typewritten manuscript, 10 pp., on file in the office of the Brooklyn Bureau of Charities).

Gives statistical and other data about twenty-five families.

Gruening, E., The Outposts of Our Empire, New York *Times,* Magazine Section, Sept. 30, 1936.

A current review of Puerto Rico written by a well-known authority on Latin America, who was also at that time head of the Division of Territories and Island Possessions of the United States.

Guía hispana, Guía Hispana Publishing Co., New York, 1934.

A semiannual, classified, professional and commercial directory of Spanish-speaking people in New York City.

Halpern, I. W., J. N. Stanislaus, and B. Botein, The Slum and Crime, Polygraphic Company of America, New York, 1934 (published for the New York City Housing Authority).

Hanson, Earl P., The Dilemma of Puerto Rico, *Science and Society,* Vol. I, No. 4 (Summer, 1937), pp. 499-511.

Hill, William E., Porto Rican Colonies in New York, 1929 (typewritten manuscript, 14 pp., on file in office of the National Urban League).

Gives interviews and summarizes conditions found in the Puerto Rican group.

Hull, H., Better Times for Puerto Rico, *Current History,* Jan., 1936.

Contains a discussion of the relief and rehabilitation program for the island.

Jones, C. L., Caribbean Backgrounds and Prospects, D. Appleton Company, New York, 1931.

Kennedy, Louise V., The Negro Peasant Turns Cityward, Columbia University Press, New York, 1930.
> An indispensable book for the student of the migration of the Negro to the large city.

Kiser, C. V., Sea Island to City, Columbia University Press, New York, 1932.

Lynsky, Elizabeth M., Porto Rico and the United States, U. S. Paulist Press, New York, 1931.

McCord, J. E., and Associates, Types of Farming in Puerto Rico, University of Puerto Rico, Division of Agricultural Economics, Bulletin 41, 1935.

McHugh, Rose J., Social Welfare among the Spanish-speaking People, National Conference of Catholic Charities, Report of the Sixteenth Session, 1930.

Manning, Caroline, The Employment of Women in Puerto Rico, U. S. Department of Labor, Women's Bureau, Bulletin 118, 1934.

Meyerhoff, H. A., Geology of Puerto Rico, University of Puerto Rico, Monograph, 1933 (see especially Chapter IX).

Mixer, Knowlton, Porto Rico, History and Conditions, Social, Economic, and Political, Macmillan Company, New York, 1926.
> Still one of the valuable studies about the island.

New York City, Department of Health, Health Center Districts, 1935.
> A handbook of statistical reference data for the five-year period, 1929-33.

——— Department of Health, Quarterly Bulletin, Vol. II, No. 4, 1934.

——— Housing Authority of, Real Property Inventory, 1934, Polygraphic Company of America, New York, 1934.
> A detailed study of housing in the entire city. Data for boroughs published separately.

New York State Crime Commission, A Study of Delinquency in a District of King's County, J. B. Lyon, Printers, Albany, 1927.

O'Connor, F. W., Concern of the United States with Tropical Diseases, *American Journal of Public Health,* Jan., 1935.

——— Animal Parasitism in Connecticut and Adjoining States, *Yale Journal of Biology and Medicine,* July, 1936.

Pan American Sanitary Bureau, Health Suggestions for Travelers in the Americas, Publication No. 96, Washington, Aug., 1934 (distributed by U. S. Public Health Service).
> Contains a discussion of parasitical diseases for the layman.

Pattee, S., Distress in Puerto Rico, *Commonweal*, Sept. 25, 1935.

Porto Rican Diet (mimeographed study, 1930, 13 pp., on file in office of Welfare Council, New York).
>A report prepared by the New York Nutritionists (Luise D. Addiss of the Charity Organization Society was chairman of the group) for the use of social workers who are interested in helping the Porto Ricans with their nutrition and health problems.

Porto Rico, What It Produces and What It Buys, U. S. Department of Commerce, Bulletin No. 785, Government Printing Office, 1932.

Puerto Rican Emergency Relief Administration, First Report (J. R. Bourne, Administrator, Aug. 19, 1933, to Aug. 31, 1934), Bureau of Supplies, Printing, and Transportation, San Juan, P.R., 1935.
>Contains a description of the distress of the Puerto Rican people and the problem of relief.

——— Tariff Problems of Puerto Rico (D. DeGolia, Director, Tariff Survey Division), Bureau of Supplies, Printing, and Transportation, San Juan, P.R., 1935.

Puerto Rican Reconstruction Administration, Census of Puerto Rico, Bulletin No. 1, Number and Distribution of Inhabitants, Government Printing Office, 1935.

Puerto Rico, Commissioner of Health, Annual Report, 1934-35 and later years.

——— Commissioner of Labor, Annual Report, 1934-35 and later years.

——— Department of Agriculture and Commerce, Puerto Rico, Commercial and Industrial, Bureau of Supplies, Printing, and Transportation, San Juan, P.R., 1934.

——— Department of Education, Rural Life in Puerto Rico, Bulletin No. 1, n.d.

——— Governor of, Annual Report, 1935-36 and other years.

Reed, Ruth, The Illegitimate Family in New York City, Columbia University Press, New York, 1934.

Rice, John L., Health Problems among the Puerto Ricans in New York City (a mimeographed study, 1934, 9 pp., on file in office of the Department of Health, New York City).

Robison, Sophia M., Can Delinquency Be Measured?, Columbia University Press, New York, 1936.

Rodrigues, A. P., A Report Dealing with Labor Statistics, Cost of Living, Housing Conditions, and Craftsmanship of Workers in Puerto Rico for the Fiscal Year 1933-34, Department of Labor of Puerto Rico, Bulletin No. 6, Bureau of Supplies, Printing, and Transportation, San Juan, P.R., 1935.

Sedition and Students, *Time*, March 23, 1936.

Survey of the Public Educational System of Porto Rico, made under the direction of the International Institute of Teachers College, Columbia University, 1926.
> This report discusses the results of mental tests administered to school children in Puerto Rico.

Taylor, Paul S., Employment of Mexicans in Chicago, *Journal of American Statistical Association*, June, 1930, p. 206.
> Numerous other studies have been made by the same author about the Mexican worker in the United States.

Thompson, Warren S., Population Problems, 2d ed., McGraw-Hill Book Company, Inc., New York, 1935.

U. S. Congressional Record, Senate Vol. LXXX, Part 6, April 23, 1936, pp. 5925-27.
> Contains the statement of Senator Tydings at the time he presented his bill for the independence of Puerto Rico. Also contains statements and statistical data about the alleged election frauds on the island.

U. S. Department of Agriculture, Report of the Puerto Rican Experiment Station, Mayaguez, P.R., 1935.

U. S. Public Health Service, Filariasis in Southern United States, Hygienic Laboratory, Bulletin No. 117, Government Printing Office, June, 1919.

Waterman, W. C., Prostitution and Its Repression in New York City, 1900-31, Columbia University Press, New York, 1932.

Welfare Council, New York City, The Puerto Rican Community Committee, Reports.
> The majority of these reports were made in the year 1930, and consist of mimeographed minutes of meetings of the committee. There are also a number of reports of discussions given to the meeting by members on problems connected with the migration and the group in New York. Material on file in the office of the Welfare Council.

Wood, Edith E., Slums and Blighted Areas in the United States, Federal Emergency Administration of Public Works, Housing Division, Bulletin No. 1, Government Printing Office, 1935.
> An excellent survey of housing studies in New York and other cities.

Index

Index

Adjustments required of migrants, 4, 59, 82, 127-55
Age composition of island population, 28
Agriculture: as background of migrant, 12-17, 26-27, 70; disinclination to engage in, in U.S., 75
Air and sunshine, 109, 126
American occupation: improvements in health conditions under, 39; improvements in education, 43, 61; growth in population since, 46; conditions under, 155n
Amoebic dysentery, 120
Amusement places, 129
Anti-American feeling, 21
Apartments: *see* Buildings

Baths, 38, 99, 106
Beds, renting of, 103
Begging on streets, 130
Behavior: problem, 137; influence of conditions on island still affecting, 140, 141
Beverly, Governor, 48
Birth control, outlook on island, 47-49
Birth rate on island, 30, 33, 46
Boundaries and census tracts, 93, 94, 170
Brazilians, dislike for Puerto Ricans, 149
British West Indies: Negroes resent workers from, 82; syphilis, 124
Brookings Institution report, excerpts, 39, 46
Brooklyn: *see* New York City: Brooklyn
Buildings: residential and dwelling writs in New York, 91ff., 167ff., *table;* rentals, 98, 100, 107, 127; age, condition, vacancies, equipment, 99; in Brooklyn area, 106; *see also* Housing
Building service, 72
Business, types in Harlem, 128; *see also* Occupations

Campos, Pedro Albizu-, 21, 153
Cancer mortality, Puerto Rico and U.S., 40n

"Carriers," dysentery spread by, 121
Cartoon, 92
Case study, 6, 159
Catholic Church: opposition to birth control, 48; Puerto Ricans usually affiliated with, 151
Catholic Church for Spanish-speaking people, 129
Cats, possible source of parasitical infestation, 122
Census tracts, 93, 94, 170
Cervantes, the, 129
Charity organizations, nonsectarian, influence, 153; *see also* Welfare agencies
Children: large proportion of, on island, 28; growing excess of births, 30; infant mortality, 42, 111-14, 123; illegitimacy, 49, 142; progress in school dependent upon health, 122; undernourished, exposed to disease, 123; use of coffee, milk, need for cod-liver oil, 125; affection for, care of homeless, 142; characteristics, relation of poverty to success in school work, 146; activities, 148; *see also* Juvenile delinquency
Chinese: *see* Orientals
Churches, 129, 152; *see also* Catholic Church
Cigar makers, 91n
Citrus fruits, 15
Clark, V. S., quoted, 39, 46
Climate of New York, adjustment to, 60
Coffee, 15; children's use of, 125
Cold, fear of, 81, 103
Color: fusion of Negro, Spanish, and Indian strains, 23; of migrants, 60; discrimination against worker on basis of, 79; discrimination in matter of housing, 92; less discrimination on island than in U.S., 142, 150; complex problem of, 150; white Puerto Rican adopts American attitude, 151
Communist organizations, 154
Community service: *see* Welfare agencies
Construction workers, 74

Cotton, 15
Crime, 91, 131-41; court records for slum areas, 131ff.; racial percentages for delinquents, 137; homicide rate for Puerto Rico, New York, and the U.S., 140
Crowding and doubling up, 89, 101-3, 143
Cuba: sugar industry, 15n; plan to deport foreign workers, 50
Cubans, difficulties with Puerto Ricans, 83

Death rate: on island, 30; for selected diseases, 40; from tuberculosis, 40, 47, 110-16; infant mortality, 42, 111-14, 123; in Manhattan and Brooklyn, *table,* 112; in Harlem, *chart,* 113; for five-year period, *table,* 114
Delinquency, 91, 131-41, 165; court records for slum areas, 131ff.; racial percentages, 137
Democratic party, work for Puerto Rico, 154f.
Dependency of Puerto Ricans, 83-87
Depression: economic distress, 44; net movement back to island during, 55; effect upon employment, 72; dependency of migrants, 83-87; stimulates interest in housing and public works, 90
Desertion, 143
Diarrhea, 42, 110; chronic, 121
Diet: *see* Food
Discriminations, 79, 80, 81
Diseases: chronic diseases of the *jíbaro,* 26; death rate for selected, 40 (*see also* Health; Tuberculosis); parasitical, 42, 49, 78, 110, 120-23; causes of infestation, 122
Doctors, scarcity on island, 42
Dogs, possible source of parasitical infestation, 122
Domestic and personal servants, 26, 70; wages, 36; migration, 62; decline in jobs, 73; placements, 75; handicaps, 77
Domestic relations, disintegrating influences, 141-44
Dominican Republic, 50
Doubling up, in housing, 101-3, 143
Dysentery, 120

Economic status of worker, 70; as shown by dependency, 83-87

Education: Puerto Rico, 43-44; opportunity for educated native in development of, 61; illiteracy of migrant, 145; little done to provide instruction for low-income group, 146
Election frauds, 140
Emergency Relief Bureau of New York City, estimated number of Puerto Rican families on relief, 84
Employment: *see* Occupations
Employment agencies, 72; *see also* Puerto Rican Employment Service
English language: *see* Language
Enteritis, 42, 110
Environment: abrupt change from rural and tropical island to industrial city, 3; adjustments to, create social problems, 4, 59, 82, 127-55

Families: birth rate, 30, 33, 46; character of family group, 86; loyalties and affections, 86, 142; overcrowding, 89; increase in number of, 100; doubling up, 101-3, 143; size, 101; number of, according to size, 103; disintegrating influences, 141-44
Family, U.S. census definition of, 102
Farmers and farm laborers, 27; *see also Jíbaro*
Farms, 14
Fascism, protest against war and, 154
Females: *see* Women
Fifth Avenue Hospital, 129
Filariasis, 121
Filipinos, Mexican attitude toward, 83, 150
"500-acre law," 14n, 46n
Food: dependence upon outside sources for, 16, 46; inadequate and improper, 26, 42, 78, 124-25
Ford, James, *Slums and Housing,* 91
Foreign-born, crime rates, 140

Garment workers, 75
Girls: *see* Women
Grocery business, 71, 128
Gruening, Ernest, 45
Guitars, 148

Haiti, 50
Halpern, I. W., and others, *The Slum and Crime,* 91, 131; quoted, 133, 134
Harlem: *see* New York City: Harlem
Harlem, 1934, 90f.

Index

Hat making, 75, 143
Health: conditions on island, 39-43; relation of housing to, 37, 89; parasitical diseases, 42, 78, 110, 120-23; handicap of disease in obtaining employment, 78; problem in New York City, 109, 110-26; contact with infected persons, 110; health center districts, 111-14; tuberculosis, 114-20; general health conditions, 123-24; problem of diet, 124-25; see also Death rate; Diseases
Health districts, 97ff., 165
Heckscher Foundation for Children, 129, 148
Home conditions: relation of unsatisfactory, to school difficulties, 146; see also Families; Housing
Home Relief Bureau, 130; wages below level of, 74, 75; relief grants, 74n; demonstrations at, 130, 154
Homework, 75
Homicide, rate for Puerto Rico, New York, and the U.S., 140
Hookworm, 42, 78, 110, 122; possibility of eliminating, 49
Hospital beds, shortage, 119
Housing: Puerto Rico, 37-39; in New York City, 89-109; evidence of crowding, 89, 101-3; relation to health and moral life, 89; discrimination against migrants on basis of color, 92; general characteristics in Harlem, 97-101 (see also Buildings); Brooklyn area, 103-6; general characteristics, 106-7
Hurricanes, 12, 18, 19; of 1932, 44

Illegitimacy, 49, 142
Illiteracy: on island, 20, 43; of migrant, 145
Immigrant groups: influence of mores of mother country, 139; Puerto Rican lacks strength of European stocks, 158; see also Puerto Rican
Income, per capita, 44
Independence: agitation of Puerto Ricans for, 5, 20-22; would involve restriction of immigration, 5; possible results if granted, 20, 21; Tydings Bill, 22; organization for, 148; demonstrations for, 153
Independent hand trades, 26
Indian strain in race, 23

Industrial ability, 18, 26, 43, 73, 76-83, 159
Industrial school, Puerto Rico's need for, 76
Industrial training, needed to meet conditions in New York, 77, 144
Infant mortality, 42, 111-14, 123
International Cigar Makers' Union, 79
International Ladies' Garment Workers' Union, 79
Intestinal parasites: see Diseases, parasitical
Italians: Puerto Ricans get along well with, 82; high ratios of delinquency, 136

Jamaica, 50
Jews, Puerto Rican conflict with, 92
Jíbaro: money wage, 16; economic condition, 25; food, diseases, 26; not able to migrate, 62
Jones Act, 20
Juvenile delinquency, 91, 131-41, 165; court records for slum areas, 131ff.; racial percentages, 137

Laborers, unskilled: *see* Workers
Labor market, competitive: migrant poorly equipped to enter, 43; see also Occupations
Lamp shades, 76
Land: shortage, 12, 13, 15; concentration, 46n
Land Utilization Committee of New York, survey of housing conditions, 90
Language: Spanish universally spoken, dislike of English, 44, 144; importance of knowledge of English, 77, 144; important in determining area of settlement, 96; colored Puerto Rican's desire to speak only Spanish, 150
Latin-Americans, differences between groups, 149
Laundry work, 72, 74
Leadership by prominent Puerto Ricans needed, 147
Legitimacy, less important in family relations on island than in U.S., 142
"Little Spain," 130
Living costs, 36
Living standards: on island, 33, 37, 42; obstruct birth-control movement, 49; low, in New York, 110

Lodginghouse, 102
Lymphangitis, filarial, 121

McHugh, Rose, 85
Maladjustments, social, 131-41
Malaria, 40, 110, 120
Malnutrition, 124
Manganese ore, 18
Manhattan: *see* New York City: Manhattan
Marcantonio, Vito, 153
Medical examination: not required for migrants, 110; X-ray examinations for tuberculosis, 116; *table,* 117
Medical service, community, 126
Meinhard Memorial Health Center, 122; clinic, 117
Men: find work less readily than women, 52, 73; left temporarily on island, 142
Mexicans: migration problem, 4; attitude toward Filipinos, 83, 150
Middle Atlantic States, Puerto Ricans in, 57
Migration of Puerto Ricans: problems involved, 3, 5; background of migrants, *see* Puerto Ricans; compared to imigration of Negroes and Mexicans, 4; may soon be accelerated, 4, 29, 159; freedom to enter U.S. without restriction, 5, 29, 50, 52; sources of information, 6; related to island's population problem, 11, 20, 28, 49-50; possible effect of independence upon, 20; by way of towns and cities, 25, 62; wages a factor in, 34; to city rather than to rural districts of U.S., 43; bearing of health conditions on island upon, 39, 41, 42; relation of economic conditions to, 45, 55; movement to U.S., 51-65; motives, 51-52; ease of movement, 52; size and year of movement, 53-55; places of settlement, 55-59, 62-65; transportation facilities, 56, 156; tendency to move North and East, 57; sex and color of migrants, 60; social classes represented, 61; small part of total to U.S., 65; only a partial solution of problem, 87; scarcity of published material, 163
Milk, scarcity of, on island, 42
Moral life, relation of housing to, 89
Mortality rate: *see* Death rate
Mosquito bite, filariasis conveyed by, 121

Moving pictures: New York theaters, 129; Argentine and Mexican films, 147
Music, 148

Nationalist movement: *see* Independence
National Tuberculosis Association, 163
Navy Yard: *see* New York City: Brooklyn
Needlework, 18, 19, 76, 143
Needleworkers, 26, 27, 70; earnings, 36; migration, 62; decline in jobs, 73; placements, 75
Negroes, American: migration problem, 4; attitude toward Puerto Rican, 82, 151; Puerto Rican's attitude toward, 82, 149, 150, 151
—— Puerto Rican: Negro strain in race, 23; little discrimination against on island, 24; settle with Spanish-speaking people, 96; tuberculosis, 125; in East Harlem, 127
Newspapers, 129
New York City: migration to, *see* Migration; Puerto Ricans an important group in certain sections, 3; adjustment required of migrant in, 4, 59, 127-55; belief in wealth to be earned in, 51; Puerto Rican settlement is pull to people on island, 56; transportation facilities from island to, 56, 156; sex and color of migrants, 60 (*see also* Color); social classes represented, 61; low economic status of Puerto Ricans, 61, 83; concentration in certain areas, 62-65, 164; Bronx, Greenpoint section, 64; Puerto Rican worker and his family, 67-159; problem of needy migrants a predepression condition, 84, 85; housing, *see* Housing; Morningside Park, Washington Heights, 92; migrants affect health conditions, 111; social maladjustment, crime and delinquency, 131-41; disintegrating influences affecting family, 141-44; need for vocational training, 144-46; recreational and social outlets, 147-51; reaction to religious and political influences, 151-55; position may be less secure than on island, 157; method and materials used in selection of areas having large Puerto Rican population, 163-66; boundaries and census tracts, 170

―――― Brooklyn: Puerto Ricans in, 62; boundaries of statistical area, 63n; Puerto Ricans on relief, 84; relief cases, 84, 85; area with large Puerto Rican population, 103-6; housing, 103-7; mixed racial groups, 104; unfavorable environmental influences, 134; census tracts, 171

―――― ―――― Navy Yard district: Puerto Ricans settled in, 61, 64, 91; a "poor neighborhood," prostitution, 107; crime and delinquency, 134; problems of domestic relations, 142

―――― ―――― Red Hook-Gowanus district, 111; a "sore spot" area, 114

―――― Department of Health: X-ray examinations, 116; case-finding program established at Meinhard Clinic, 117; shortage of hospital beds, 119; Meinhard Memorial Health Center, 122; program for treatment of venereal disease, 124

―――― Harlem section: tendency for Puerto Rican to settle in, 4, 61; occupations and employment, *see* Occupations; group conflicts, 82; Puerto Ricans on relief, 84; unemployment, 85; area with large Puerto Rican population, 91-97; *chart,* 93; boundaries and census tracts, 94, 170; Spanish-speaking racial groups, 95, 164; population density, 96, 102; general characteristics of housing, 97-101; Central Harlem health districts, 97ff., 170; crowding, 101-3; increase in number of families, 102; high infant and tuberculosis mortality, venereal diseases, 111; "sore spot" areas, 114; closer view of settlement, 127-31; East Harlem settlement, 127ff.; parks, shops, 128; institutions, color and customs of Spanish-speaking countries, 129; night life, 130; crime and delinquency, 131ff.; unfavorable environment for girl, 143; social barriers of island continue, 147

―――― Manhattan: Puerto Ricans in, 62; boundaries of statistical areas, 63n; housing, 89-103; Lower East Side, 98ff., 107; census tracts, 170; *see also* New York City: Harlem

New York City Housing Authority, 90

New York Real Property Inventory of 1934, 90, 96, 97, 98, 100, 102

New York State: Puerto Ricans living in, 58; Department of Labor study of homework industries, restrictions upon homework, 76; Crime Commission, *A Study of Delinquency,* 134; excerpt, 135

New York State Crime Commission, 107

Night life in Harlem, 129, 130

Nuestra Señora de la Medalla Milagrosa, 129

Nurses, trained, scarcity on island, 42

Occupations: lack of experience in industrial work, 18; migrants poorly equipped for, 18, 43, 73, 76; types available on island, 26-28, 70; professions, 61, 71; and employment opportunities, 69-88; where and how migrant finds work, 70-76; trades, 71; placement by Puerto Rican Employment Service, 72-75; for unskilled labor, 74; handicaps in obtaining work, 76-80; many migrants have made satisfactory adjustment, 80; other factors related to employment, 80-83; need for statistical information, 159; *see also* Wages

O'Connor, F.W., quoted, 121

Orientals, Puerto Ricans dislike, 83, 149

Panhandling, 130

Parades, 153, 154

Parasitical diseases: *see* Diseases

Philanthropic service: *see* Charity organizations; Welfare agencies

Physicians, scarcity on island, 42

Police, attitude toward Puerto Ricans, 139

Political influences: migrants' reaction to, 153-55; parades, nationalist demonstrations, 153

Political parties on island, 21

Political sponsorship of social clubs, 148

Ponce, "Massacre," 22n

Postal service, 71

Poverty: bearing on migration, 45; among Puerto Ricans in New York, 61, 83; characteristic of Harlem community, 130; *see also* Puerto Rico: economic conditions

Prensa, La, 92, 129
Prize fighting, 148
Professional classes: in Puerto Rico, 61; in New York, 71
Prostitution, 107
Protestant and nonsectarian organizations, influence upon migrants' religious attitude, 152
Puerto Rican: racial intermixture, 23; religion, 48, 146, 151-53; referred to as colored, 79; referred to as Spanish, or foreigner, 80; characteristics: quick temper, sensitiveness, 81; practice of sharing, 86; loyalties and affections, 142; characteristics of children, 146; mixture of cultural elements, 150; physical characteristics, *see* Health
Puerto Rican Community Committee, 69, 85
Puerto Rican Employment Service in New York: placements, 72-75; handicaps reported, 76, 77
Puerto Rican Service Center of New York, 128
Puerto Rico: as background of migration, 5, 9-65; agitation for independence of, 5, 20-22, 148, 153; resources, 11-22; geography, 11; climate, 12, 18; topography, 13; agriculture, 12-17, 26-27, 70; farms, leading crops, 14; mineral resources, 17, 18; water power, 18; present government, 20-22 (*see also* American occupation; United States); political parties, 21; education, 43-44; election frauds, law requiring simultaneous casting of ballots, 140; work of Democratic party for, 154f.; Department of Labor employment service, *see* Puerto Rican Employment Service
———— economic conditions, 16, 33-47, 62; land shortage 12, 13, 15, 46*n;* dependent upon outside sources for food, 16, 46; effect of American tariff, 16; system of growing money crop to exchange for food, 17; industries, 18; obstacles to industrial development, 19; pressure of population upon resources, 20, 23, 33, 46-47; the *jíbaro,* 25 (*see also* Jíbaro); occupations, *see* Occupations; wages, 33-36, 51 (*see also* Wages); subsistence level, 36; housing, 37-39; conditions under American occupation, 39, 43, 61, 155*n;* aggravated by the depression, 44-45; bearing upon migration, 45, 55; rapid economic development, 46; financially unable to provide for its people, 87
———— population, 23-33; migration related to, 11, 20; area per capita, 12, 13; pressure upon resources, 20, 23, 33, 46-47; composition, 23; rural, 25; growth, 28, 50; large proportion of children, 28; birth rate and death rate, 30, 33, 40, 46; density, 31-33, 46, 50; alternatives for relieving pressure: birth control, 47-49, migration, 49-50
———— social problems: illiteracy, 20, 43; anti-American feeling, 21; health, 39-43, 110; crime rate compared to that of U.S., 140
Pulmonary tuberculosis, 41, 116; *see also* Tuberculosis

Racial contact: *see* Italians; Negroes; Orientals; Social relations
Racial groups, Spanish-speaking, in Harlem, 95, 164
Racial intermixture, 23
Real Property Inventory, 90, 96, 97, 98, 100, 102
Recreation: inadequacy of facilities, 135; recreational and social outlets, 147-51
Red Hook-Gowanus district: *see* New York City: Brooklyn
Refrigeration, 99, 106
Relief, public: on island, 45; bearing on movement back to island, 55; allowances, 74*n;* poor economic status shown by dependency, 83-88; New York agency, relief strikes, 130
Religion: influence on birth control, 48; profess to be Catholics, 146; migrant's reaction to, 151-53
Rentals, 100-101, 107; unsatisfactory housing indicated by law, 98, 127
Restaurants, Spanish, 129
Restaurant work, 71, 72
Riggs, Francis E., 21*n*
Robison, Sophia M., 164
Rosario, Professor, 23; quoted, 24
Rural worker: *see* Jíbaro
Salaries: *see* Wages

San Juan, 59
Schistomiasis, 121
Servants: *see* Domestic and personal servants
Sewing: *see* Needlework
Sex of migrants, 60
Shops, 128
Slum and Crime, The (Halpern, I. W.), 91, 131; excerpt, 133, 134
Slum Clearance Committee, 90
Slum conditions: on island, 37; in New York, effect upon health and morals, 89; relation to crime, 131
Social agencies: *see* Welfare agencies
Social and recreational outlets, 147-51
Socialists: on island, 82; attitude toward U.S., 21; sympathy for Spanish Loyalists, 154
Social maladjustments, 131-41
Social organizations, 148
Social problems created by adjustment in new community, 4, 59, 82, 127-55
Social relations, effect of mixed and congested communities on, 149ff.
"Sore spot" areas, 114
Sources of information, 6; methods and material used, 163-66
South, fear of racial discrimination in, 55
Spanish-American War, Puerto Rico acquired as result of, 20
Spanish language: *see* Language
Spanish-speaking people in New York City, 64, 91*n*, 92ff.; professions listed in commercial directories, 71; average wage, 72; racial groups in Harlem, 95, 164; not inclined to educational advantages, 145; relations between educated, and Harlem group of Puerto Ricans, 147
Spanish War, migrant's sympathy with Loyalist cause, 153, 154
Sprue, 121
Statistical areas of concentration, 62-65, 164
Statistical information, need for, 159
Stores, 71
Storms, hurricanes, 12, 18, 19, 44
Strikes: workers' attitude toward, 82, 154; before home-relief agency, 130
Sugar industry: in Puerto Rico, 14; in Cuba, 15*n*

Sunshine and air, 109, 126
Syphilis, 124

Tariff, American: effect upon Puerto Rico, 16, 19; possible result of sudden withdrawal, 20
Teachers, opportunity on island, 61
Teatro Hispano, 129
Tenements, old-style, 91
Theaters, New York, 129
Tobacco, 15, 19
Toilets, 38, 99, 106
Toreador, El, 129
Trades, 71
Trade unions, discrimination against Puerto Ricans, 79, 82
Trade winds, 12
Transportation facilities, 56, 156
Tuberculosis: death rate, 40, 47, 110-16; a handicap in obtaining employment, 78; case-finding studies, 86; among migrants in New York, 114-20; X-ray examinations, 116; *table,* 117; related to adequacy of facilities for treatment and segregation, 119; worse in New York than on island, for colored migrant, 125
Tydings Bill, 22

Unemployment, 85
Unions, discrimination against Puerto Ricans, 79, 82
Union Settlement, 128, 148
United States: Puerto Rican a citizen, 3, 20, 79, 94f., 156; freedom to enter without restriction, 5, 29, 50, 52; Puerto Rico the most unhappy possession, 20; reaction to independence movement, 22; movement to, 51-65 (*see also* Migration); belief in high money wage to be had in, 51; number of Puerto Ricans living in, 53; Middle Atlantic states, 57 (*see also* New York State); Puerto Rican migration relatively unimportant, 65; problem of free entry, 78*n;* Puerto Rican's resentment toward, 145, 154, 158; migrant looks to, as escape from economic conditions on island, 156
Urban League, no organization among Puerto Ricans similar to, 163

Venereal disease, 111, 124
Vivaldi, J. M., quoted, 73
Vocational training, need for, 144-46
Voz, La, 129

Wages: in Puerto Rico, 33-36; on island and in U.S. compared, 34; Department of Labor survey of wages and cost of living, 35; a motive for migration, 51; attract migrant to urban centers, 56; in New York, 72; below levels of WPA and Home Relief Bureau, 74, 75
Washington: *see* United States
Water power, 18
Welfare agencies, 6; Puerto Rican case load in depression years, 84, 85
Welfare Council of New York, 69, 163; forms Puerto Rican Community Committee, 85
West Indian: inability of Puerto Ricans to compete with natives of other islands, 50; American Negro's attitude toward, 82; attitude toward Orientals, 149. toward American Negroes, 150

White strains, pure: in race, 24; in migrants, 61
Women: occupations, 27, 75, 76 (*see also* Domestic and personal servants; Needleworkers); find work more readily than men, 52, 73, 142; decline in number placed in jobs, 73; need for warm clothing, 125; delinquency, 107, 133; lack of protection in lower-income group, protection in upper class, 142; older than husbands, 142; problem of the working mother, 143
Workers, unskilled: positions secured, 74 (*see also* Occupations); economic difficulties not solved by migration, 88, 158
Workers Alliance, 154
Working mother, 143
Worm infestations, 121
WPA: migrant unwilling to attend WPA schools, 145; wages, 74*n;* Puerto Ricans' wages below level of, 74, 75

Yankee imperialism, Latin-American complaints against, 154